INCURABLY HUMAN

Written and Illustrated by Micheline Mason

Dedicated to:

Marsha Forest, Jack Pearpoint, Judith Snow,
John O'Brien, and Herb Lovett
who flew in as a team,
crashed through our British reserve
and, in their generosity,
gave us the language and the tools of inclusion.

© Micheline Mason 2000
ISBN 1 870736 38 9

Incurably Human

© Micheline Mason 2000
ISBN 1 870736 38 9

wORking Press
47 Melbourne Avenue
Palmers Green
London
N13 4SY

wORking Press publishes books by, for and
about working-class artists and writers.
For further details and a publications list contact
working_press@compuserve.com
http://ourworld.compuserve.com/homepages/working_press

wORking Press is a member of the
Federation of Worker Writers and Community Publishers

Layout Richard McKeever
Cover Design Nancy Willis

Printed by Adept Press
273 Abbeydale Road Wembley
Middx. HA0 1TW
Tel: 020 8998 2247 www.adeptpress.com
a commercial litho printing company staffed
mainly by deaf people and run as a co-operative.

About the Author:

Micheline Mason was born in 1950 near London, England. At the age of four days, she was diagnosed with a condition called Osteogenesis Imperfecta, or Brittle Bones, and was immediately christened in hospital in expectation of her imminent death. Fifty years later she is a writer, artist, disability equality trainer, and a teacher within the Re-Evaluation Counselling Community.

She is a mother of a sixteen year old daughter who looks set to upstage her on every front, (except any form of cleaning up).

Ten years ago she joined with other disabled people, parents and allies to form the 'Alliance for Inclusive Education', a campaigning organisation which brings the voice of the 'excluded' into the heart of the debate on what kind of societies we are trying to create through our education system.

Contents

Permissions

The author would like to thank the following publishers for permission to reprint excerpts from their publications:

Inclusion Press for *What's Really Worth Doing & How to Do It* by Judith Snow; *Inclusion! The Bigger Picture* by Marsha Forest and Jack Pierpoint; *All My Life's a Circle: Using the Tools CIRCLES, MAPS and PATH* by Marsha Forest and Jack Pierpoint; *The Careless Society*, by John McKnight; *Celebrating The Ordinary* by O'Brien, O'Brien and Jacob.
Granta for *False Dawn –The Delusions of Global Capitalism* by John Grey.
Macmillan Books for *The Man who Mistook his Wife for a Hat* by Oliver Sacks.
Souvenir Press for *Everyone Belongs* by Kenn Jupp.
Routledge for *Disability Politics* by Jane Campbell and Mike Oliver.
The Manchester Coalition of Disabled People for *Dangerous Woman* by Sue Napolitano.
Highfield Junior School for *Changing Our School*.
The Circles Network for their *Annual Report 1996*.

The author has made every attempt to get permission for all other quotations.

Incurably Human

Introduction

As a good Catholic child, born with a physical impairment, I struggled to understand the story of St. Bernadette and the miracles at Lourdes. When a favourite auntie visited the grotto on my behalf, she brought me back a plastic bottle filled with "water" and told me to sprinkle it all over my "poor little legs" and to pray to Jesus to make me better.

Dripping Holy Water on my Poor Little Legs

Well, I tried to please her and my mum, did a bit of sprinkling and praying, but after a few nights of this, when not much improvement could be seen, I got bored and did something unmentionable with the water and one of my dolls.

Somehow I just could not get behind the idea that there was something "wrong" with me that Jesus had missed on the "production line", but could remedy at a later date. It didn't fit into my understanding of things, but at ten, I did not have the ability to argue the point.

A few years later, at my "special" school, I remember one of the care-staff loudly telling me that I should never give up hope because one day doctors would find a cure for my affliction, and I loudly told her that I did not want to be "cured". I remember this incident because of the utter disbelief this statement caused amongst all the non-disabled people present, and the delight this statement caused amongst my disabled friends. The school decided that I had "The Wrong Attitude" and that I should indeed go to Lourdes so that Jesus, the Virgin Mary and St. Bernadette could sort me out.

Curiosity persuaded me to join the "Handicapped Children's Pilgrimage to Lourdes", mostly because it would mean flying on an aeroplane which, at the time, seemed unbelievably exciting.

Lourdes was full of ill and disabled people wanting to get "better", supported by hoards of non-disabled people with the same idea. I found it utterly depressing. I started praying for non-disabled people to be "cured", but cured of what? It was still hard to find the words.

Disabled people have a joke about Lourdes. We come out of the Holy Water with a brand new set of tyres for our wheelchairs. The joke often falls very flat when told to non-disabled people. It provokes the same baffled look as the one worn by the staff members in my "special" school. Nowadays however, a few people get it, and laugh with us.

Inclusion is a concept that is not easy to "get", just like that joke. In fact, you have to get the joke to understand the real meaning of inclusion, especially as it applies to education and the "Special Education System".

I am beginning to realise that 'inclusion' is not a definable state, but a set of principles, which can be applied to anything. It is not essentially about 'disability', but about building a sustainable future for all of us. The fact that inclusion is not our current reality is because of a system, or 'model' of understanding the world which is mistaken. This model has been called the 'Cartesian Model' which understands the world as a machine which is running down, a giant clock.

This has led to the idea that we could understand how it works by dismantling it into its components, and those components into its components and so on. It is a system of thought which has led to specialisation, compartmentalisation, fragmentation, analytical thinking and related approaches to solving problems. This includes the 'medical model' of disability or behaviour. I am a living testimonial to this mistake, as are many other disabled or segregated peoples. Together with my fellow 'victims' we are able to give voice to the human effects of following this particular path. Therefore we will help create an explanation of what needs to change in our understanding of how the world works. 'Inclusion' is an imagined future based on a world view which could be called 'ecological', in which our interdependence is truly understood.

This book is an attempt to take the reader on my journey of discovery, starting from my childhood certainty that I was already fully human, and therefore not in need of a "cure", to a much later understanding that all human beings are "incurable" at our core, and that the inclusion movement is this inextinguishable flame made visible. Each chapter is like the overturning of a stone along a path - my discovery of a small piece of a picture which will hopefully one day fit together into a natural pattern. As you read it, and when you have finished it. I hope you will realise that each one of you has come along a unique path of your own, not mine. Mine may only help you shed light on your own, and give you enough confidence to continue, and above all share your discoveries with others, so that the journey feels more like an outing with friends than a lone battle against the world.

EXCLUSION HARMS EVERYONE

Exclusion Makes the World Unsafe

Most excluded people perceive that they have nothing to lose, and everything to gain in the battle to belong. Many youth consider a matter of life and death. Teenagers join gangs because they are desperate to belong - to have meaning. Even when the gangs kill, the youth join. The gangs meet their needs. Gangs are a logical response to society's failure to make teenagers feel belonging. When our youth literally die to belong, it is a searing warning for us to look hard at the system in which we live

Marsha Forest & Jack Pearpoint Inclusion! The Bigger Picture[1]

Isolation and segregation have been used throughout history as punishments. Isolating people in prison, we like to think, is a deterrent to crime, but not everyone we choose to segregate has broken the law. We have taken the same approach to deterring people from being poor, disabled, ill, mad or immoral. In the late 18th Century we built workhouses which were like prisons in order to deter the 'undeserving poor' from being idle and living on Poor-Law handouts. We also built long-stay hospitals and institutions, not unlike prisons, to house 'defective' people and 'moral imbeciles' who dared to have illegitimate children. They were built to deter other people from forming relationships with disabled children being born with the same 'defects' as their parents. The breaking of relationships between disabled and non-disabled people, and between disabled people of the opposite sex, has had a profound effect on the world in which we live today. It holds out a model of punishment, devaluing and isolation as society's response to poverty, disability, emotional or behavioural difficulties, and ageing. Because any of these things could, (and in the fullness of time probably will) happen to anyone, we all live in fear and dread of it being us.

This fear has permeated our culture to such a degree that we cannot imagine a world in which we are not preoccupied with being acceptable to others .

Not being the right size and weight, not having the right appearance and clothes, the right manners and style, high enough status, the right ideas and opinions, the right material possessions are of immense concern to us because they all seem to lead to exclusion - being 'outside', being alone.

Exclusion Harms Everybody

It is a rational human need to belong, and therefore every little exclusion, from "You can't play with us!" "Go to your room!" "We're not talking to you", to "You're fired", "You're expelled", "You're sentenced to prison", is a form of violence against the person, or group.

The reaction is as predictable as the scientific rule of energy, that force in one direction will be met by an equal and opposite force. People who experience violence become violent. They become directly violent to the perpetrator of the original violence (hit right back), or become violent towards someone smaller and weaker than themselves (bullying), or become violent towards themselves - the most common reaction, especially amongst females. Depression, eating disorders, drug taking and suicide are the most common examples.

People who have experienced exclusion tend to form alienated gangs and cliques in an attempt to belong to something, many of which have anti-social or criminal cultures. Any society which creates an 'underclass' of people who are excluded by poverty, racism, or segregation, will have to deal with the resulting violent reaction

Exclusion harms both the victim and the perpetrator. Perhaps recognising the anger and resentment of the excluded, perpetrators the world over feel under siege and in need of defence - more police, more prisons, more power to expel, more locks, fences, barbed wire, security cameras, the private ownership of knives and guns, longer and stiffer sentences:

Affluent Americans are withdrawing in ever larger numbers from cohabiting with their fellow citizens into gated propriety communities. Some 28 million Americans - over 10% of the population - now live in privately guarded buildings or housing developments

'Many Seek Security in Private \ Communities'- New York Times 1995

At the end of 1994 just over 5 million Americans were under some form of legal restraint ...By the start of 1997 around one in fifty adult American males was behind bars and about one in twenty was on parole or probation.

Richard Layard, "Clues to Prosperity" financial Times 17 Feb. 1997

Out of fear, they promote a culture of blame and self-righteousness, with simplistic notions of good and bad, justifying intolerance, retaliation and revenge. In the USA where they employ one third of the worlds practising lawyers, incarceration and litigation have become the primary means of social control This culture is spreading throughout the developed world.

People Need Communities

The reason the fear of segregation is so powerful is that it is the opposite of what we need as human beings.

For all of our known existence, up until the last few decades, people have chosen to live in communities. Those communities have always been based around the extended family, tribe or clan. They have included people of all ages and operated as collaborative teams with clearly defined roles for everyone.

It is as true now as it has ever been that the relationships we have in our lives are what give our lives meaning and purpose. It is also true that communities are what keep vulnerable people safe, and there is no alternative to this. The idea that we could build caring services, which would replace the need for cohesive social communities, has proved to be false. In fact some such services are now being revealed to be magnets for people who are abusers of all kinds. No one relishes the idea of going into a hospital, or 'home' as they grow older, and no child would rather live in 'care' than at home with a real family, preferably their own. We all want to live with the people who love us, and to love them back. That's the way we are. Yet this common human need has been almost sacrificed in the name of 'progress', especially in the developed world.

The Global Economy Destroys Community

The so-called 'free-market' does not provide consumers with proper information, because the social and environmental costs of production are not part of current economic models

Fritjof Capra –The Web of Life.[2]

I am not an economist and am not going to pretend to have anything more than the crudest understanding of world-wide capitalism and the 'free-market', but I do still have some rudimentary ability to see cause and effect.

Capitalism, albeit in many different forms, is now the only economic system of any consequence throughout the world. It has spread because, in its own terms, it is very successful at creating wealth, and also because of the unremitting pace of technological developments which drive it forwards. Although capitalism has existed for a long time, until recently it was always tempered to some degree by national governments with managed economies. How these nations managed their economies was based on their history, traditions and cultures. For example capitalism in India does not have exactly the same form as capitalism in France,

Capitalists were traditionally the descendants of warlords, people who invaded lands, declared ownership, called themselves Kings and ruled by force. They created legal systems of inherited wealth and power to keep it within the family, or dynasty. These landowners built the first great factories and financed the industrial revolution. We are still used to thinking in these terms when we think of capitalism, but the picture is now very different. The traditional royalties and 'upper classes' are now board members and share-owners in huge, multinational organisations many of whom have no particular connection with any one nation, but whose operations are spread all over the world. This has partly happened because of the USA-born concept of the Free-Market. The Free-Market has as its ideal a completely unregulated flow of capital around the world, leaving 'profitability' as the only regulator of the market. There is in this idea the notion that it is 'consumer-led' and therefore a more true reflection of the will-of-the-people than any managed economy, and is therefore the only economic system worthy of 'free-men' such as Americans.

The free market destroys community because it leads to money moving around the world at an unprecedented pace, moving factories to the cheapest source of materials or labour, the country with the weakest trade unions, the countries with least financial controls, countries without social unrest, countries with better educated young people, lowest pension rights, least restrictive labour laws and so on. This leads to job insecurity and a mobile labour force, and in the West, to a loss of manufacturing industries and an unprecedented growth in service industries.

The free market effectively limits the power of national governments by the threat of the withdrawal of capital if certain policies are introduced. It is not supportive of democracy but of the over-arching power of greedy Trans-national Corporations.It is highly competitive in nature and creates therefore a highly competitive and individualistic culture. It relies on ever increasing consumerism which itself relies on creating the feeling of need for 'things', not people, through relentless advertising and peer pressure. It tends to withdraw finances from community based services into privatised services, continually espousing the power of the individual to buy what they need rather than rely on collective solutions, such as taxes and benefits.

15

The withdrawal of the social safety nets which can only be sustained by 'managed' economies, leads inevitably to more poverty and hardship for some, who will, just as inevitably be blamed for their own situation as 'welfare bums' etc. So a circle has been created from the Victorian era of the Workhouse, the 'deserving and the undeserving poor', the concept of the moral defective, and the 'belief' that the poor create poverty.

The family, as the single most important indicator of social stability, breaks down in direct relationship to the degree to which we de-regulate our economies. In the USA, Britain and New Zealand where the free-market experiment has been undertaken with greatest enthusiasm, the divorce rate has risen, the numbers of lone-parent households has rapidly increased and so has the number of children showing signs of emotional and behavioural distress. The rate of suicide amongst young people has also risen, especially amongst young black males in both the USA and the UK where they are also a disproportionately high percentage of the prison population. In fact, in the USA there are over a million young black adults locked up by the State, in their so called 'Home of the Free.'

In New Zealand, ten years of deregulation created a social underclass where one had not existed before:

The New Zealand experiment is the free-market project in laboratory conditions: uncompromising neo-liberal ideology animated a programme of radical reform in which no major social institution was left unreconstructed...It came from the perception in the Treasury that New Zealand's position as a First World country was becoming economically untenable. That in turn was a by-product of ongoing economic globalisation, particularly the emergence of highly successful modernised economies in the hitherto Third World countries such as Singapore...Immediately or shortly after the Labour Government took office in July 1984, exchange controls were abolished and the currency floated, controls on prices, wages, interest rates, rents and credit scrapped. Subsidies to exports were removed, import licences abolished and all tariffs massively reduced. Most State owned enterprises and assets were privatised. In a break with New Zealand's long standing Keynesian inheritance, full employment was abandoned as an objective of public policy in favour of the monetarist goal of price stability. These were measures of deregulation and 'rolling back the state' that corresponded closely to those adopted by other New Right Governments, particularly Mrs. Thatcher's in Britain...Uniquely in New Zealand, farming was defunded, with nearly all state assistance and protection being withdrawn in the years 1984-7. No less exceptional was the deregulation of the labour market that went far beyond the limitations on Trade Union power introduced in Thatcherite Britain. By 1991 the system of national collective bargaining had been comprehensively replaced by individual employment contracts in both the public and private sectors...An independent central bank was created with price stability as its sole objective...Public hospitals were converted into commercial enterprises and compelled to compete with private suppliers of medical care. Education was restructured, with the responsibility for the delivery of educational services devolved to local school boards. Schools levied fees for their services and were required to supplement their budgets by commercial activities. Entitlement to welfare benefits of all kinds was vigorously pruned, with the population being stratified into economic categories which determined their levels of subsidy for state services. All state services were marketized, and all of the states welfare functions reduced...Expenditure on police, courts and prisons continued to grow...The result has been the emergence in New Zealand of a social stratum that never existed when the county was burdened by a universal welfare state - an economically marginalised, socially excluded underclass of welfare dependants...One estimate puts 17.8% of the New Zealand population under the poverty line in 1991.

John Grey 'False Dawn" Granta Books[3]

The reason the family suffers so much as an institution in the 'free-market' is that it has become very difficult to financially survive as a family without two wage earners to pay the bills. This means there is no one at home to look after the children, cook decent meals, care for the elderly relatives, or support vulnerable family members when they need it. Relationships actually need time put into them for them to work, and time is what people don't have.

The need to be able to move around to find or keep work also destroys the 'extended family network' as many family members end up living faraway from each other. It is often the existence of a close extended family which makes the difference for families with a disabled child between being supported at home or institutionalised, and also for single parents to make a success of their situation.

The inherent need in any capitalist system is for new markets. There are four main routes to this - swallowing up smaller companies; moving into new geographical areas; developing new products and technologies and persuading people to sell what they once gave free of charge. Thirty years ago it would have seemed unthinkable that we would be buying bottled water, selling strips of sky (to airlines) or sending our toddlers to children's hotels whilst we go to overnight business meetings, but we do all of them now without much question. Soon we will be paying each other to smile!

The World Trade Organisation, under the leadership of such people as Michael Moore, the architect of the New Zealand Experiment, is now attempting "To write the constitution for a single global economy" (Renato Ruggerio, Director General, WTO). It is seeking to implement a multilateral agreement on investment (MAI) which would empower corporations and investors to sue governments directly for cash compensation in retaliation for almost any government policy or action, including taxation, environmental or employment regulations, which undermines profit.

The Professionalising of Care

A careful analysis of the recent areas of professional development indicates that 'unmet needs' are the growth sector of the service industry. The most recent discovery of these new 'needs' include 'tired housewife syndrome', 'six-hour retardation' (a child who is normal for the 18 hours a day not in school), 'bereavement deficit', (previously known as grief), 'incipient child abuse' (the possibility that a parent might hurt a child), 'litigative incapacity', (the lack of funds to sue others to secure equity), and 'reclusiveness', (the desire not to associate with others). Each of these new discoveries of unmet 'needs' creates a 'demand' for a new profession.

John McKnight, - the Careless Society 1995 [4]

One major development in persuading people to pay for things which were once given free is the multiplication of the 'caring professions'. The dominant approach to disability has led to many people being paid to 'fix us' or to look after those of us who cannot be fixed. Because of the now largely unacceptable historical assumptions outlined in the section on eugenics, modern day services are seen as in need of reform, to be designed on more enlightened views such as 'Care-in-the-Community'.

Inclusion however, is not about reforming paid services to make them more acceptable. Inclusionists believe that the problem we are facing is not of weak services, but of weak communities. Indeed, the current economic need for growth and national stability *depend* on more professionalised services of the type we already have because it is projected by Daniel Bell amongst others, that by the year 2000, approximately 90% of people in the developed world will be employed in the service industry:

All of the forces in our economy are now programmed to create a geometric increase in the number of professionals while the goods production sector is designed to replace the labour of Americans with machines and foreign labour. The Government must increase the GNP and 'control' unemployment....

In our drive to increase professional service 'production' there is a popular assumption that we are intensifying the good works of society. With more professionals we will kill cancer, make the criminal justice system work, learn how to teach reading, cure deafness, and give sight to the blind

John McKnight – The Careless Society [5]

Disabled people have long argued for de-professionalised, user-led services, adequate incomes and the opportunities to learn, work and participate in our local communities.

John McKnight takes this one step further, looking at the providers of services as 'people in need':

After all, they are a growing majority of people employed in modernised societies and they are an increasingly sad, alienated class of people in <u>need</u> of support, respect, care and love. Modernised societies <u>need</u> to determine how we can help these professionalised servicers while limiting their power to disable the capacities of citizens to perceive and deal with issues in political terms.

John McKnight – The Careless Society[7]

No time for living.

"Not conversing", said Eeyore, "Not first one and then the other. You said 'Hallo' and flashed past. I saw your tail in the distance as I was meditating my reply. I had thought of saying 'What?' – but of course, it was then too late".

"Well, I was in a hurry."

"No give and take", Eeyore went on, "No exchange of thought: 'Hallo – What' – I mean, it gets you nowhere, particularly if the other person's tail is only just in sight for the second half of the conversation"

From The Tao of Pooh, Benjamin Hoff [8]

The relentless pursuit of a higher standard of living has created the need for paid carers to look after unfortunates left on the sidelines, because no one else has the time to do it.

Industrialisation has speeded us up, but for whose benefit? All the rest of the living world, plants and animals, pace their lives in tune with natural rhythms. The rotation of the earth, the moon, the sun, the lengths of days and nights, the warmth or coldness of the seasons, the winds, rains and droughts of the weather – these are the factors which govern the activity of everything except ourselves. The inbuilt biological clock of birth – childhood – maturity – death is allowed to tick along without interference in all creatures, except humans.

We have realised that human beings are the most flexible of all animals, because of our enormous capacity to create new responses to situations as they arise. This is our greatest strength, but when misused has the potential for being our downfall. Economic systems such as slave-societies and feudalism, and present day class-based societies, all have the inbuilt concept of one group of people owning the labour-power of others, and therefore profiting from their work. The more they work, the more 'productive' they are, the more profit can be made.

Watches and clocks were of no great interest to most people until the industrial revolution. Before then, families worked together at home, in cottage industries or on the land. They worked during daylight, sharing tasks as they chose, for which they received a family wage. It was only with the advent of industrialisation that people were coerced to work in factories for an individual weekly wage. The steam powered machinery, artificial lighting were all inventions used to make working people more productive, and owning class people more wealthy, because they enabled them to create patterns of work which did not depend on length of daylight, or the warmth of the weather.

It is worth remembering that it took nearly a hundred years to persuade people to change their life styles, and much force was used against the widespread organised resistance of working class people.

It is still shocking to realise that in Britain, only 100-200 years ago, children as young as six were being sent to work in mines, factories and as chimney sweeps, and women were being made to work 10-12 hours a day. People have struggled hard against this, with some success, both middle-class reformers and the Trade Union Movement, have managed to moderate the excessive demands of the 'Bosses', so that these kinds of conditions would today be unthinkable – in the so called 'developed world' at least.

The means of production however, basically remain the same, and our values have gradually been shaped accordingly. People who are 'quick' are valued, people who are 'slow' are not. Much technology is invented to speed up the process of production, with the most significant being the rapid development of communication systems and information technology. It has been noted that with the use of all these inventions each one of us is several times more productive than we were a few years ago. This speeding up, living with constant stimulation has actually affected our beings far more than we realise. It has been found for example that the levels of adrenaline in our systems means that for many people, stress is no longer caused by too much pressure, but by being *slowed down*. For example the new phenomena of 'Road Rage' can be understood as an overload of stress caused by having our way blocked, being held up, or made to reduce our speed for 'too long'.

Simply being unable to 'keep up' with the general flow of things causes the process of exclusion. As the 'general flow' goes faster, so more people find themselves left behind. Even if you make a conscious decision to live your life at a slower, more measured pace, the price is often to be isolated – there is just no one at home to be with, they have all rushed off down the 'Superhighway' of Progress. Such progress has no doubt brought an improved standard of living to almost everybody, but at an increasing cost to the quality of our lives.

The challenge of inclusion is to create a pace of life in which everyone, including the 'slowest', can take part. Most of us feel that we have much less control over our time than we do, but it is an area of confusion and powerlessness for many – trying to get everything done. It makes us tired just thinking about it.

The idea of being 'unproductive' is like a demon in our heads. "I haven't done anything today!" we wail, when our whole day has been taken up listening to our troubled neighbours, washing clothes, trying to work out why our partner looks so stressed. Many of the things which are most likely to improve each others quality of life are considered to be 'doing nothing', such as thinking. Actually it is not possible to do nothing and be alive. If we could hear all the activity going on in people's heads as they sit silently staring into space, a doctor's waiting room would become deafening.

There is much evidence to show that doing less can lead to being more effective. Many disabled people are 'slowed down' by their impairments, but this can often mean that, because of the greater effort required, actions are more selective and less impulsive. My non-disabled father for example, never went out of the front door only once on his way to work.

He would run out of the front door, feel in his pocket for his car keys, discover them missing, run back in the house, up the stairs, pick up the keys from his bedside table, run downstairs, out of the door, get in his car, start it up, get out, run back in for his glasses / pipe / book / money / post etc., run out, get back in the car, get out, run back in, kiss my mum and tell her what time he would be home for dinner, run out, get back in the car and drive off. I, on the other hand, as it takes me ten minutes to get out of the front door and into my wheelchair-accessible van, never leave the house without everything I might need. In fact I keep my coat, keys, money, diary and remote control for my van, on or in my wheelchair at all times. These energy saving tactics lead to whole habits of thinking and being.

Many eastern philosophies seem to be about the art of thinking before you act. In fact they are more than that. They are about becoming 'aware' of the present, inside and outside yourself, and learning to be sensitive to circumstances. In the Tao of Pooh, Benjamin Hoff calls this the 'principle of minimal effort'. As far as I understand it, it means that there is a natural flow to life which we can either work with, or against. If we pay enough attention to what is happening around us, we will learn to 'feel' the 'flow' and be able to add our energy to it. This way we become part of a natural movement in which desirable things seem to 'happen' without much effort. If we do not pay this attention however, we get caught up in straight-line, combative or egotistical effort that goes against the nature of things, and this causes us to make mistakes, get hurt, and wear ourselves out. The ever increasing speed of our lives is fobbing us of the time to 'become aware', so many of us get busier and busier whilst achieving less and less of satisfaction. Or we keep adding force to our (wrong) efforts to try and make them work – but instead create a bigger resistance.

Many people who are currently left on the sidelines because of their inability to keep up, and those who love them, have been tuning in to the 'natural flow', becoming painfully aware of the different paths that are being followed.

I think it is so hard when we have to spend so much time trying to do things adults think are important, like work or getting ready. Why can't we have time to really talk to each other? It is so hard

23

*because I need people who can help me and they are not always
there when I want them. So we need time when we are altogether
so thatwe don't have to keep making arrangements.*

Maresa Mackieth, speaking at an Inclusion Conference, Lambeth 1999

These people bring to the inclusion movement the gift of 'slowness',
in a world going too fast.

Eugenics Shapes Our Thinking

The current situation for disabled people and other devalued groups
cannot be understood without an exploration of the past. In particular,
it is vital to understand the mistaken assumptions and distortions of
ideas which have created a pseudo-science called Eugenics.

Eugenics appears to account for inequality as an inevitable condition
of humanity. It began with the attempt to replace superstition and religion
with objective reason based on actual evidence – the scientific approach.
Not a bad thing in itself, but unfortunately open to manipulation by the
powerful in a class-dominated society to justify their privileged position.
For example, soon after the publication of 'The Descent of Man' by
Charles Darwin, his followers began to misapply his theory of natural
selection to race and class. Darwin said that the genes which were most
able to adapt to their environment would survive where others would
fail – the 'Survival of the Fittest'. His followers however, thought that
this only applied to pre-civilisation:

*At the present day it does not seem possible for natural selection
to act in any way so as to secure the permanent advancement of
morality and intelligence, for it is indisputably the mediocre, if
not the low, both as regards morality and intelligence, who succeed
best in life and multiply the fastest*

A.R. Wallace, 'The Action of Natural Selection on Man'[9]

Although there was nothing to suggest this in Darwin's work, his
followers argued that mankind consisted of several different species of
higher and lower orders, evident in different races and social classes.
They believed, that with natural selection no longer operating, the poor
(lower orders) were multiplying at a faster rate than the rich and that
this was a dangerous situation:

Among savages the vigorous and sound alone survive, amongst us the diseased and enfeebled survive as well... with us thousand with tainted constitutions, frames weakened by malady or waste, brains bearing subtle and hereditary mischief in their recesses, are suffered to transmit their terrible inheritance to other generations, or to spread it through a whole country

William Rathbone Gregg 'Enigmas of Life' 1872 [10]

They believed society would benefit by selective breeding. Eugenics was a word coined by Francis Galton and the society which bore this title quoted his definition of it on the cover of 'Eugenics Review:

Eugenics is the study of agencies under social control that may improve or impair the racial qualities of future generations, whether physically or mentally.

It is interesting to note that they included the white working class in their definition of 'race'.

Members of the British Eugenics society were small in number but powerful, including very influential figures such as George Bernard Shaw, Professor Julian Huxley, Marie Stopes, Cyril Burt, Winston Churchill, Major Leonard Darwin, (son of Charles Darwin who was the President from 1911 to 1929), and DH Lawrence:

If I had my way, I would build a lethal chamber as big as the Crystal Palace, with a military band playing softly, and a Cinematotograph working brightly; then I'd go out in the black streets and the main streets and bring them all in, the sick, the halt and the maimed; I would lead them gently, and they would smile me a weary thanks; and the band would softly bubble out the 'Hallelujah Chorus'.

D.H. Lawrence 1908 –The Letters of D.H. Lawrence Vol.1.

At one end of the scale they isolated themselves (Good Stock) and only married within the class, encouraging each other to do their duty and have lots of babies, whilst at the other extreme they passed laws which would allow them to segregate 'cripples, the feeble-minded and moral defectives' (Bad Stock) into single sex institutions to prevent them from breeding at all.

In Britain the 'Mental Defectives Act' of 1913 allowed local authorities for the first time to remove 'defective' people, including children, from their homes and incarcerate them in institutions. Doctors were given the job of deciding who these defectives were, and several official categories, ranging from Cretin to Moral Defective were introduced, each one supposedly identifiable by a battery of objective tests.

The racial blood shall not be poisoned by moral disease. The guardians of social life in the present dare not be careless of the happiness of coming generations, therefore the criminal is forcibly restrained from perpetuating his vicious breed

Jane Hume Clapperton – 'Scientific Meliorism' 1885 [11]

Eugenicists confused the effects of poverty with heredity. For example they did not know that rickets was caused by poor nutrition, but noticed that only working class children seemed to be affected. From their observations, they developed the theory of 'differential fertility' - that the lower classes were more 'fecund', had more babies, and that more of their babies were defective with each succeeding generation. If this were not stopped, the whole of society would eventually decline.

For many eugenicists the incarceration of defective people was not enough. They thought that institutions were very costly, and some of the inmates managed to escape. In Europe and the USA, another solution was promoted. The first law providing for the sterilisation of feeble-minded, insane, syphilitic alcoholic, epileptic , and criminal individuals had been passed in Connecticut in 1896. Kansas followed in 1903, Ohio, New Jersey and Michigan in 1905. In California alone over 6000 people were deprived of their fertility. Denmark and Switzerland also passed eugenic sterilisation laws whilst Sweden carried out as many sterilisations in one year as were carried out over the whole period in the USA.

In Britain the Eugenics society, encouraged by the Report of the Joint Committee of the Board of Education and the Board of Control, who had found that:

Mentally deficient parents create centres of degeneracy and disease which welfare work can never reach

We began concerted lobbying for our own Eugenic Sterilisation Bill, but it was never enacted. Interestingly it was the intervention of geneticists who were by then beginning to have a greater understanding of human biology who probably caused enough doubt to stop it happening:

Sterilisation of defectives can never bring about results of practical value. Meanwhile ill-considered handling of the problem may cause unnecessary suffering for a small section of individuals, but that is all it will do. If we sterilise a few, we may avoid having to feed a trifling number of defective people. If we go too far, and particularly if we adopt compulsory sterilisation, we shall make an unnecessarily large number of people unhappy.

Gunnar Dahlberg - 'Race, Reason and Rubbish', New York 1943

By the early 1940s Hermun Muller discovered that it was probably mutagens in the environment which were the real cause of the growing number of congenital impairments and auto-immune system diseases, but this likelihood has not yet replaced the pseudo-science of inheritance in the consciousness of most people. It is true that it is no longer acceptable to state the more obvious classist or racist beliefs of the early part of the century, but many of today's practices, strongly defended by doctors, educational psychologists, social scientists and many others are direct descendants of the original Eugenic laws, values and beliefs. Take for example I.Q Testing, still used to identify level and type of intelligence or 'learning difficulty' as a basis for placement in a segregated school. One of the designers of the Stanford-Binet Intelligence Test had this to say about the desirability of 'tracking' or 'setting' in U.S. schools, or the placement of certain children in separate classes or schools:

Among labouring men and servant girls there are thousands like them (feebleminded individuals). They are the world's 'hewers of wood and drawers of water'. And yet, as far as intelligence is concerned, the tests have told the truth...No amount of school instruction will ever make them intelligent voters or capable voters in the true sense of the word.

...The fact that one meets this type with such frequency among Indians, Mexicans and Negroes suggests quite forcibly that the

whole question of racial differences in mental traits will have to be taken up anew and by experimental methods.

Children of this group should be segregated in special classes and be given instruction which is concrete and practical. They cannot master, but they can often be made efficient workers, able to look out for themselves.

Lewis Terman- The Measurement of Intelligence, 1916

Terman's book, 'The Measurement of Intelligence', was used for decades in teacher training.

In Britain, Cyril Burt promoted the use of I.Q. Tests with the same eugenic conception of humanity:

During the past 40 years work with standardised tests has conclusively established (I) that a general factor underlying all forms of mental efficiency may plausibly be assumed,(ii) that this factor can be assessed with reasonable accuracy by both group and individual testing, (iii) that the differences in intelligence as thus defined are due largely to the individual's inherited constitution.

Cyril Burt – 'Intelligence and Fertility' London 1946

Cyril Burt's own peers exposed the fact that his evidence was faked. The tests he had claimed to perform on the parents of his subjects, thus 'proving' the inherited and fixed nature of intelligence, had never been carried out. He was so convinced of the innate superiority of his own class that he did not feel the need to prove his point. Despite his exposure, I.Q tests have never lost their use as a tool of social control.

Segregation is 'Kind'

In order to persuade ordinary people, particularly parents of 'defective' children to agree to a eugenic programme, they had to convince them that it was the kindest thing to do. This was a myth which they also had to create in order for people to pay for the institutions and their upkeep through voluntary donations. They did this primarily by propaganda films such as 'Heredity in Mankind" in which all the inmates of an institution were dressed up in pretty clothes and sat on a lawn in the sun, next to kindly looking nurses, or shown exercising or being trained in 'simple manual tasks, with a voice-over saying

> *These poor people are happier safe in their colonies than they would be at large in the world....Once they are born, we must do the best for them, but how much better for society if they had never been born at all.*

Heredity in Mankind – The British Eugenics Society

Like all propaganda, in order for it to work, the real voice of the real people had never to be heard. The institutions were closed to the public, even relatives, who were only allowed access on special 'open' days. Inmates who had learnt to read and write before they came to the institutions, had their letters censored:

> *When we were in the classroom we used to write home every week. After we had written a letter the headmistress passed them all on to the matron so she could read them, and she used to cross off all the things we weren't supposed to put in. We had to put it that we liked it there , and everybody was happy, and everything that was really lies. We couldn't put any of our true feelings into a letter. If we had written anything bad about the place they were bought back to us and we had to write them again, leaving out those bad things. Then they were sent back to the matron and sealed down and sent off. I used to write to my father and my grandmother. And I used to get letters back saying they were thrilled that I was so happy, but my letters were all lies.*

Mary Baker, Halliwick Home for Crippled Girls, 1930s – Out of Sight [12]

Disabled People are a Burden we Cannot Afford

The overall image that was created of disabled people was of being a burden which society could not afford. This reached its peak in Germany in the late 1930s when Hitlers' Third Reich issued leaflets comparing the costs of caring for a disabled child with that of a 'normal' child, proclaiming them to be 'Useless Eaters'. He did this to persuade parents to send their disabled children to hospitals to be 'treated', but from where it was understood that they would not return. Some parents did this, but the practice was stopped eventually by public outcry and rioting in the streets in 1942. Hitler had underestimated people's compassion in his openness about what they were doing, a mistake he did not repeat later with the Jews and other victims of his Eugenic Final Solution.

'Medical Science' Masks Prejudice and Ignorance

When I first arrived at Halliwick the nurse took me into this bathroom and she stripped me off completely. She cut my hair short, right above the ears. And then I was deloused with powder of some description. Then they put me in a bath and scrubbed me down with carbolic soap. It was very degrading to me and I felt as though the end of the world had come...I didn't know what to do, had no idea what I was going to do. But it was huge and it was lonely that place. And I felt really lost, and I thought 'what am I going to do with no-one to love me?'.... The next morning you were given a number and you had to remember it. My number was twenty-nine and when I got up and went to wash, my towel and flannel had my number on them. Twenty-nine was engraved on all my hairbrushes and things with a red hot poker-like thing. Everything I owned had a marking of twenty nine so I can never forget that number....and if matron wanted you she just called you by that number. We never had names. We were just numbers there.

Mary Baker, Halliwick Home for Crippled Girls, 1930s – Out of Sight [13]

Doctors, many of whom were themselves Eugenicists, were happy to take on the role of deciding who should go to these institutions, partly because they then had a great deal of captive material for their study and experiments. It is shocking now to realise how much of what was said to be scientific fact was actually doctors making guesses based on misconstruing observed appearances or characteristics of their patients. For example, one doctor noticed similar facial and bodily features of one group of people often incarcerated in long-stay mental handicap hospitals, and observed that they resembled the facial features of the Mongolian peoples of the East. He then made a connection between the racist and eurocentric beliefs of the time, that the further away from Europe you got, the less intelligent you were, and pronounced these people to be throw-backs to our primitive ancestral past, labelling such patients as 'Mongols'. It is worth remembering here that although Mendel had done his experiments with peas by then, the physiology of genetics and the discovery of DNA did not happen until the 1950s.

It was assumed at that time that a person's physical appearance was a reliable indication of their mental capacity. Any kind of physical deformity or problems of co-ordination or speech was thought to mean that the person also could not think. Deaf people who used signed language instead of verbal language were locked up in mental-handicap hospitals along with people with cerebral palsy. They were all the same, defective and incapable.

There was also a great confusion between intellectual impairments or learning difficulties and the ability to think and feel. This led to the idea that such people were not fully human and therefore did not have the same human needs as others, so what would have been considered cruel if applied to a 'normal' person was quite acceptable when done to a disabled person e.g. separating them from their families as young children. Use of dehumanising descriptions such as ''cabbages' or 'vegetables', helped to numb people's compassion towards such victims.

Training not Education

As it was thought that disabled people were basically ineducable, the emphasis within the institutions was to train them to do simple work. This could help them make an economic contribution to their own upkeep, not by giving them a wage, but by using the proceeds of their labour to help cover the costs of running the institution.

The institutions began to be divided into 'schools' for the young people, and 'workshops' for the adults:

On the day that I left school I was told that I was going into the mat shop and that was that. There was no choice at all. We had twenty odd looms in our mat shop at the workshops, big thundering things they were. And the common run of the mat maker was that you stood winding yarn round a steel rod and thumping the big heavy baton down and bang the rows up together. We did that then hour after hour, year after year, lifetime after lifetime

Ted Williams, Sharrow Lane Workshops 1930s – Out of Sight [14]

The notion that some children were ineducable persisted right up to 1974 when responsibility for the last group of children, labelled as 'Severely Sub-normal' was transferred from the Health Service to the Education System.

Eugenics Lives On: The Medical Model of Disability

Young people were interviewed who are effectively being 'warehoused' in residential provision: they have little opportunity for making friends, being involved in their local community, or doing anything meaningful during the day. To a large extent the scope for any personal development had ceased.

Joseph Rowntree Trust ''Findings', September 1999

Although there is now far better understanding of human biology and the affects of certain conditions upon us, covert eugenic policies still dominate medical practices. The sterilisation of the poor, the disabled, those with genetic impairments; pre-natal screening and termination of 'defective' babies, differential abortion laws which allow termination of such babies up until full-term; the persistence of segregated institutions and 'group homes' and 'villages' for people with impairments; the disproportionate labelling of black and ethnic minorities with psychiatric problems, criminal tendencies, 'learning difficulties' or 'challenging behaviour'; the false correlation between poverty and poor educational attainment; the promotion of punitive social policies which blame single-mothers for our nations decline - all of these still happen.

Residential institutions still exist for adults and for children; local authorities can still 'place' people in them against their will; people still confuse illness with impairment; doctors and other professionals still label us and act as gatekeepers to services.

It is still assumed we cannot think, especially people who are labelled as having learning difficulties, or cannot speak verbally.

People still think that children are disruptive or aggressive because they are bad, and come from bad families; people still think we don't (and shouldn't) have sex, marry or have children; people still think we cannot work and be productive.

People still think our 'Special Needs' are related to treating, or ameliorating the effects of our impairments, and that our 'ordinary needs, can be ignored. At the time of writing this book (1999) local Education Authorities still use these arguments to use their power to place disabled children into segregated schools against their wishes:

> *We are persuaded by the evidence that David's special educational needs require provision in a small group environment with specialist teaching suited to David. We are of a view that David's learning needs, in relation to his literacy and numeracy, require intensive support throughout the curriculum....We accept that David is developing his independence skills and he requires on-going age appropriate vocational assistance and guidance to build further on these skills.*

> *However the evidence did not persuade us that educating David at Knockbreda High School with the extra provision of a classroom assistant for 20 hours a week and part-time teaching for five hours a week, as requested by Ms McKibben (David's mother) would meet David's special educational needs.*

> *In coming to this decision we carefully considered Ms Kibben's clear preference for a mainstream education for David and David's recorded wishes to attend Knockbreda. On the evidence submitted we accept that Tor Bank (special) School could meet David's special educational needs.*

Special Educational Needs Tribunal decision, January 1999 [15]

David's mother is currently (December 1999) under the threat of a prison sentence if she does not comply with this order.

The Human Genome Mapping Project

> *If I could snap my fingers and be non-autistic, I would not - because then I wouldn't be me. Autism is part of who I am.*

> *Aware adults with autism and their parents are often angry about autism. They may ask why God created such horrible conditions as autism, manic depression, and schizophrenia. However, if the genes that caused these conditions were eliminated there might be a terrible price to pay. It is possible that persons with bits of*

these traits are more creative, or possibly even geniuses..... If
science eliminated these genes, maybe the whole world would be
taken over by accountants.

Temple Grandin – The Anthropologist from Mars [16]

Human genetic engineering is a continuation of the eugenicist belief
in social control through manipulation of the gene pool. Sold to the
public as a possible source of treatment for people suffering from genetic
diseases such as cystic fibrosis, its potential for permanent alteration of
the gene pool is what really excites scientists. Therapy for living people
is likely to be limited to those few diseases or conditions caused by a
single gene, and even then one which has to be repeated as often as the
affected cell replaces itself. However the possibility of germ-line 'therapy'
which involves altering the genes in the male/female sex cells has the
potential to eradicate certain genes forever. Furthermore the technology
has the potential for the real dream of the geneticists – human
'enhancement' through un-natural selection, once the genome has been
mapped,i.e. every gene identified and 'labelled'. This mass gathering of
information through a hugely expensive international project, The Human
Genome Mapping Project, will allow us to know the hidden genetic
potentialities of any embryonic human being. This not only includes
genetic abnormalities but also genetic pre-dispositions to conditions such
as cancer or heart disease. Coupled with the twin technologies of selective
abortion and genetic engineering, it does not take a genius to see where
this could be leading. Even if its' potential turns out to be greatly over-
estimated, the attempt, and all its hype, still distracts from the real
problems before us.

The Breaking of Relationships

About two hours after Danny was born, the neonatologist came
into my room and told me I had a 'Mongoloid son'. I didn't take
it very well. My husband Alfredo and I went out to the nursery to
look at Danny. The nurse thought she was being well intended
and said "Do you want your son at the window where everyone
can see him, or do you want him away from all the other babies
where nobody can see him?" It was like she threw a bucket of
cold water at us, and we couldn't believe she was asking us that.

Alfredo turned all different colours and said "Of course we want him there. Why shouldn't he be there? He's like all the other babies.

Carmen Ramirez

If you were to ask anyone what it is that gives their life meaning, most would say it is the people they love and who love them. Childcare theorists virtually all agree that the bonding process between a new-born infant and his/her primary carer is crucial to the child thriving. Without this even where all physical needs are met, babies "wilt" and sometimes die.

Disabled people suffer a form of violence that is unrecognised. Current interventions from nearly all professionals and service providers have the effect of breaking natural relationships between disabled people and everyone else. When this happens in early childhood, the consequences are devastating both for the child, and for society as a whole. Let us examine many common practices around young disabled people.

Even before a child is born interventions serve to damage the relationship between the child and her/his mother. In this period of time, before the baby has a look and a feel, a sound and a name - before "it" becomes a real, unique individual, the relationship is at its most vulnerable. Pre-natal testing, with its expected result being termination of any "imperfect" foetus, is offered routinely to pregnant women. The world, through its white-coated spokespeople, carries a value judgement into the new relationship, which can completely destroy it, even before the mother and child have met. The mother, at this point, may be armed only with what she has learnt about disabled people from charity posters, special school busses, and the popular press, and everything, including these kind doctors who are looking after her, is telling her that the world does not want any more disabled babies, and that she would never be able to cope. Her fear may well lead her to agree to end that babies life.

After birth, interventions rarely have such a dramatic effect because everything is balanced against the reality of the child, and the positive feelings which that child may evoke in his/her carers. Even so, the relationship begun with the child is likely to suffer many blows and manipulations along the way to adulthood.

Many parents of disabled children talk of the moment of disclosure - the time they were told that their baby had an impairment. They talk about being isolated from the rest of the ward, curtains, embarrassment, clinical language they did not understand, an aura of sadness, disappointment and commiseration. Parents still tell of suggestions from medical staff that they should leave the baby behind in the hospital and "forget" about it. "Bereavement" counselling is offered although the baby is not dead, to help the parents grieve for the "proper" baby they did not have. Then they are sent off home to come to terms with their tragedy.

Now totally pulled in two, parents often begin to love their child, but hate the impairment, as society has taught them to do. They see the impairment as the cause of societies' rejection and desperately start to search for people who can take "away" or "mend" the impairment. Many willing people will turn up anyway, with therapies and programmes which hold promise of doing just that. Some parents do not wish to follow this path, and resist the efforts to medicalise and "manage" the child, but these parents are often labelled unco-operative and irresponsible. Either way, little is done to help parents to relax and feel proud of their disabled child, or to give parents an understanding of the oppression they are inevitably facing because of having a child who is de-valued and denied basic human rights within the current legal framework. They know they have to fight for everything they get, but no-one tells them why, or makes the connection with disabled adults who are struggling together to end this kind of mistreatment.

Perhaps more importantly, no one takes the burden of this fight off the shoulders of the already exhausted parents and leaves them space and energy to play, and have fun with their children.

Enjoyment is the last thing on the agenda when talking about parenting and disability, but without this the child feels they are the cause of a lot of stress and anxiety for the people who love them, which of course is another erosion of the child's self-esteem. (Disabled children often learn to be bright and cheerful and flippant about their own needs as a way of attempting to cheer up their parents.)

It is inevitable that all this damages parent's ability to love their child unconditionally. In the same way as a doctors favourite patients are her/his success stories because they validate the doctors skills and concern, and make her/him feel powerful and fulfilled, or a teachers favours pupils who are the ones who clearly learn and grow under the influence of their teaching, the relationship between professional and "client" is relative to results. When a parent is turned into a therapist, or an educator for their disabled child, the child may well feel that the love, which they so desperately need, is conditional on their performance in the "getting better" game. Likewise, the parents may also feel that approval from the "real" professional depends on their child's co-operation and "improvement" - *"The Portage worker is really nice, and she will stop coming if you don't learn to pick up this cup ...."*

Where is the child in all this? – the unique individual who came into the world expecting a fanfare and champagne, only to find tears and disappointment? For a disabled child the world can seem very strange indeed. Lots of adults paying attention to "something" of which the child is completely unaware. The child's sense of self always includes what others call their "impairment" as an integral part of their being. The only "them" they have ever known. If they are in pain, they probably want it to stop. But apart from that, the child is like any other, driven to learn and become itself - a whole, new person with a body, mind and soul.

A disabled child, even with major difficulties in moving, speaking or processing information, will seek to gain control over self and the environment according to their own inner motivation. Through endless interaction with others and the material world, through play and experiment, trial and error, laughter and tears, every child develops their personality, skills, and sense of belonging in the world. When other people assist the child to initiate interactions, the child learns to expect co-operation from others, and confidence in her/his self. Play and therapy are not the same thing. Play is about the child's goals, therapy is about the adult's goals. The more impairments a child may have, or the greater degree of those impairments, the higher is the level of professional intervention, the less will the child "play" and the more they will be directed by others - and the less ability will they have to protest or get away!

Many "programmes" for young children, for example Dolman-Delaccatto therapy involve forced manipulation of the child's limbs for several hours a day, by adults the child may not even know. It is difficult to know how the child can cope with this without "shutting off", going numb, or giving up in some way. The "medical" model of disability attacks ones' relationship with oneself because the assumption is made that the impairment is the enemy, but in reality the impairment is part of the person, and only the person can themselves choose to separate them without feeling torn apart. So uninvited intervention, however well meaning, is a form of violence to the inner being.

If the self is thwarted in its development, and the impairments become the major factor in planning a child's life, and the parents love for their child has been eroded by the negativity surrounding their child, then it is easy to understand how parents can be persuaded that sending their child away to specialists is the best thing for everyone. And even if parents do not think it is the best thing, it doesn't matter because the State still has the power to segregate disabled children and place them in separate schools and units, some residential, up until the age of 19, without the agreement of the parents (Section 316,1996 Education Act.) For many more seriously impaired children, this separation can begin as early as two years old.

Whatever the hoped for outcome of such a drastic measure, the immediate effect is to create an artificial environment for young disabled people, away from their brothers and sisters, from their local friends, and sometimes even from their parents. The idea that you can remove people from each other in order to teach them how to relate to each other, is patently absurd. Clearly relationships are not the goal of "special" education. In reality the bringing together of any group of people on the basis of common difficulty, is not a natural thing to do. People choose friendships on the basis of common interests and complimentary needs. Children in special schools, especially where the common difficulty is of communication, find it impossible to form mutually fulfilling peer relationships and are forced to relate instead to adults - Adults who do not love them and who are paid to be with them. The loss of natural relationships has never been acknowledged as the price disabled people pay in the name of 'service provision'.

The Outside-In Approach

Children and disabled people have one thing in common, our inner-worlds are considered invalid. If you are both a child and disabled you have an almost insurmountable problem to overcome - experts!

I remember going to a pre-school playgroup for children with "special needs". I went with my daughter who was then aged about four, and a friend of mine with her recently adopted disabled child who was three years old. The group was held in a child development centre and was run by someone with an "ist" on the end of her name.

The atmosphere was hushed, the children very quiet. They were all sitting near, or propped up by a parent, in a circle on a mat on the floor. We innocently joined them and the session began. The "ist" was the cheerleader, as we did round of fun-but-therapeutic activities. I can only recall two. One was the repetitive erection of a tall tower of bricks in the middle of the circle, over which each child was carried in turn, and some part of his/her body was knocked into it, sending the bricks flying amidst a noisy "Wheeee!" and clapping from the adults present.

Micheline

The other was a "walk" in which a procession of children, each "pushing", whilst being led or held up by its parent, some kind of wheeled object, whilst the cheerleader banged a drum and sang. They went out the door, along a corridor, into another room, round in a circle, and back to the mat. By this time two children were crying, one very angrily, and at least one other had gone to sleep.

My daughter decided to start imitating the "ist", trying unsuccessfully to initiate a few activities of her own, but by then tea and biscuits was the agenda item and the adults were not going to be distracted. Afterwards, I realised why I had found this whole event so disturbing; *the children had not made one single decision of their own.* It was the outside-in approach.

Donna Williams is a young woman is autistic. She has written two books about her experience of living with autism ('Nobody Nowhere' and 'Somebody Somewhere') and in an interview for BBC Television she discussed all the professionals in her life who had studied her, read books by other professionals about autism, and to her mind, invented a picture of who she was based on their own perceptions of the world, not hers. She said that they had never understood that she, and other autistic people, has each built a unique system of understanding the world. She said that the only way to make a real connection with her was to sit with her, with all preconceptions and judgements put aside, and to try to know and understand her system. Then, she said, after a few years, you might get somewhere.

The principle of a child centred Pedagogy is, of course, relevant to all young people. The US. Highscope Project, the most successfully researched programme into the importance of early intervention in children's lives advocates an approach called SOUL: Silence, Observation, Understanding and Listening, which reduces the chance of interrupting children's play. SOUL has the purpose of helping adults to become partners in the endeavours of children. This concept of partnership is fundamental to the concept of inclusion.

At the moment, many children experience abandonment by adults, or over-intervention (as in the playgroup). When I took my daughter to an open-day at a potential secondary school, the Headteacher said: "We are willing but ignorant."

It was the best thing he could have said to us. It meant to me that we would be expected to play an active part in the planning of her school-life.

It is one of the biggest misconceptions about including children (or adults) with special needs into schools or communities that people don't have enough 'training'. What they usually mean is that they want a formula, designed by 'experts', based on the medical model, which they can apply to people with particular impairments or difficulties, to make them better. This is the result of the 'professionalising of care'. The last thing anyone thinks is that they can ask the person concerned what help they need and how to give it. If the person has no form of communication, then those people who are closest to them can be of great help.

The Medical Model Prevents Learning

You appear to be very good at maths, above average, so, as you obviously don't have a problem with maths we are going to cut down on your maths lessons and give you more physiotherapy instead

Teacher to a pupil at Ravenswood school for children with the Severe Learning Difficulty label [17]

One of the most insidious forms of breaking relationships happens to children who are given labels which include the letters 'p', 's' or 'm' (Profoundly, Severely or Multiply). These young people are very likely to find themselves locked into a system based on ideas from paediatrics and child-development theory. This theory states that 'normal' children follow a straight line of development following a consistent pattern of steps or 'milestones' within a broadly similar time-scale. E.g. reaching - grasping - pincher movement - holding - manipulating - dropping an object at will etc. Diagnosis of a disability or learning difficulty usually means that doctors have become aware that a child is not progressing along this line as one would expect. It is then assumed that the child needs adult intervention to 'assist' their passage, and programmes are designed to 'teach' the child the steps they should be taking, in the correct order. Because the order is considered to be essential (one CANNOT jump over steps), the pace of learning is tightly controlled:

When the child can consistently show us that she can differentiate between red and blue, then we can add some more colours.

Quote from a teacher in a Language Unit

or *"our learning goal for all the children in this class is that they can turn towards sound"*

**Teacher in a school for children with
Severe Physical or Learning Difficulties.**

This leads inevitably to age-related levels of function defining the child - *"She has a mental age of five"*.

People who are disabled, or who live closely with disabled people know that this concept of development has little to do with real children who have physical or intellectual impairments. Real people are far more complex and individual than that.

The main flaw in the theory is that it takes no account of the fact that there is more than one way to do, or learn anything. Many disabled children develop different, unique strategies to cope with, get round, overcome, or side step blocks and difficulties which are in their way. It can take time to create these alternative paths, but having done this, they carry on their way.

If you pour water over a pre-formed shape which has one, sloping, channel which leads directly to the edge of the shape, the water will naturally follow the path of least resistance and flow quickly into the channel and down, off the edge of the shape. If however the shape is flatter, and has more bumps and grooves, the water will meander and form many small islands and rivulets whilst it finds its way to the edge. It may 'fan out', reaching its destination quickly in some areas but swirling about slowly in others. This is much more like the development of disabled children - unless it is prevented by well-meaning adults.

The effect of this level of 'structured learning' on the 'inner' child, can only be guessed at. Proponents and practitioners of 'Facilitated Communication' have defied the straight line theory of development by discovering the ability to recognise and choose symbols, letters and words in children and adults who were considered to be functioning at infancy levels. The communications which have come from the young people have confronted the world with the uncomfortable possibility that locked inside each child is a whole, thinking, feeling human being, unable to make themselves heard by a world which was not 'listening'.

Funding Failure

The medical model concentrates its resources on trying to make us do the things we cannot do, usually at the expense of the things we can do. Because of the confusion in many peoples minds between illness and disability, there is little distinction between things which can be cured (for which it is appropriate to try), and things which cannot be cured:

When I first saw (Rebecca) - clumsy, uncouth, all-of-a-fumble - I saw her merely, or wholly as a casualty, a broken creature, whose neurological impairments I could pick out and dissect with precision: a multitude of apraxias and agnosias, a mass of sensorimotor impairments and breakdowns, limitations of intellectual schemata and concepts similar (by Piaget's criteria) to those of a child of eight. A poor thing, I said to myself, with perhaps a splinter skill, a freak gift, of speech; a mere mosaic of higher cortical functions, Piagetian Schemata - most impaired.

The next time I saw her it was all very different. I didn't have her in a test situation, 'evaluating' her in a clinic. I wandered outside, it was a lovely spring day, with a few minutes in hand before the clinic started, and there I saw Rebecca sitting on a bench, gazing at the April foliage quietly, with obvious delight. Her posture had none of the clumsiness which had so impressed me before. Sitting there in a light dress, her face calm and slightly smiling, she suddenly bought to mind one of Chekov's young women - Irene, Anya, Sonya, Nina - seen against the backdrop of a Chekovian cherry orchard. She could have been any young woman enjoying a beautiful spring day. This was my human, as opposed to my neurological, vision.

As I approached, she heard my footsteps and turned, gave me a broad smile, and wordlessly gestured. 'Look at the world', she seemed to say 'How beautiful it is'. And then there came out, in Jacksonian spurts, odd, sudden, poetic ejaculations: 'spring', 'birth', 'growing', 'stirring', 'coming to life', 'seasons', 'everything in its time'. I found myself thinking of Ecclesiastes: 'To everything there is a season, and a time to every purpose under heaven. A time to be born and a time to die; a time to plant, and a time.....' This was what Rebecca, in her disjointed fashion was ejaculating - a vision of seasons, of times, like that of the Preacher. 'She is an idiot Ecclesiastes', I said to myself. And in this phrase , my two visions of her - as idiot and symbolist - met, collided, and fused. She had done appallingly in the testing - which, in a sense, was designed, like all neurological and psychological testing, not merely to uncover, to bring out deficits, but to decompose her into functions and deficits. She had come apart, horribly, in formal testing, but now she was mysteriously 'together' and composed.

Why was she so de-composed before, how could she be so re-composed now? I had the strongest feeling of two wholly different modes of thought, or of organisation, or of being. The first schematic - pattern-seeing, problem solving - this is what had been tested, and where she had been found so defective, so disastrously wanting. But the tests had given no inkling of anything <u>but</u> the deficits, anything, so to speak <u>beyond</u> her deficits.

They had given me no hint of her positive powers, her ability to perceive the whole world - the world of nature, and perhaps of the imagination - as a coherent, intelligible, poetic whole: her ability to see this, think this, and (when she could) live this; clearly <u>was</u> composed and coherent, when approached as something other than a set of problems or tasks........

It was perhaps fortunate that I chanced to see Rebecca in her so-different modes - so damaged and incorrigible in one, so full of promise and potential in the other - that she was one of the first patients I saw in our clinic. For what I saw in her, what she showed me, I now saw in them all......

During the intervening months (between my first seeing her in April, and her Grandmothers death that November) Rebecca - like all our 'clients' (an odious word then becoming fashionable, supposedly less degrading than 'patients'), was pressed into a variety of workshops and classes as part of our Developmental and Cognitive Drive (these too were 'in' terms at the time). It didn't work with Rebecca, it didn't work with most of them. It was not, I came to think, the right thing to do, because what we did was drive them full-tilt upon their limitations, as had already been done, futilely, and often to the point of cruelty, throughout their lives. We paid far too much attention to the defects of out patients, as Rebecca was the first to tell me, and far too little to what was intact, or preserved. Rather suddenly, after her Grandmother's death, she became clear and decisive. 'I want no more classes, no more workshops,' she said. 'They do nothing for me. They do nothing to bring me together'. And then, with that power for the apt model or metaphor I so admired, and which was so well developed in her despite her low I.Q. she looked down at the office carpet and said:

'I'm like a sort of living carpet. I need a pattern, a design, like you have on that carpet. I come apart, I unravel unless there's a design'.......... 'I must have meaning' she went on. The classes, the odd jobs have no meaning......What I really love', she added wistfully, 'is the theatre'...........

Oliver Sacks - The man who Mistook His Wife for a Hat [19]

The goals of the medical model have been handed down from generation to generation without much rational appraisal of whether they are either possible, or desirable. The original institutionalising and training of poor or 'defective' people coincided with the spread of taxation. In her book 'Sex and Destiny (1984), Germaine Greer notes that:

The beginnings of systematic taxation prompted a gush of self-pity as the affluent classes began to nurse the suspicion that they were being pillaged to support degenerate idlers

and quotes the poet Matthew Arnold on the subject of the children of the poor:

To bring people into the world, when one cannot afford to keep them and oneself decently and not too precariously is .... by no means an accomplishment of the divine will or a fulfilment of nature's simplest laws ... but contrary to reason and the will of God

Matthew Arnold, Culture and Anarchy, London 1869.

Although the medical model is more concerned with the 'deserving poor', its original goals were the same as those of the Workhouse - to train as many people as possible to be independent and contribute to their own financial upkeep. However, when mixed with the eugenic goal of fertility control, it led to the limited notion of people contributing to the costs of their own segregation and 'services'. This led to employment within sheltered workshops and day centres, many of which exist to this day, and which are still filled with ex-pupils of 'Special Schools:

> *Our teachers did not prepare us for anything. They had no vision of us being able to do real work in the community. In the back of their heads they expected us to be going to segregated workshops for the rest of our lives*

People First of Canada 1996

Eugenics may have been driven underground, but sometimes ideas in the unconscious can wreak more havoc than those exposed to the light of conscious reason.

The medical model is like a veil before our eyes upon which is a colourful painting . It has an attraction and coherence of its own, and is understandable when its historical development is known, but it prevents us from seeing reality, with terrible consequences:

We put all our time and energy into trying to solve the wrong problems.

Micheline

Notes: Section One

1 Marsha Forrest and Jack Pierpoint. *Inclusion! The Bigger Picture*, Inclusion Press 1989

2 Fritjof Capra, *The Web of Life*, Harper Collins 1996

3 John Grey, *False Dawn – The Delusions of Global Capitalism*, Granta Books 1998

4 John Mcknight, *The Careless Society – Community and Its Counterfeits*, Basic Books 1995

5 Ibid

6 Ibid

7 Ibid

8 Benjamin Hoff, *The Tao of Pooh*, Methuen 1982

9 Germaine Greer, Quoted in *Sex and Destiny*, Secker Warberg 1984

10 Ibid

11 Ibid

12 Steve Humphries and Pamela Gordon, *Out Of Sight* Northcote House 1992

13 Ibid

14 Ibid

15 From a personal communication

16 Temple Grandin, quoted in *The Anthropologist From Mars*, Oliver Sacks Piccador 1995

17 From a personal communication

18 Oliver Sacks,*The Man Who Mistook His Wife for a Hat* Piccador 1986

THE INCLUSION MOVEMENT

The People

The creative energies of four different groups of people have come together in a movement for social change. This movement has the potential to transform the world in which we live. Some of us think it is unstoppable.

The four groups of people are parents of disabled children, disabled people including those once labelled 'mentally handicapped'; young people, and courageous professionals who have been led to rethink their own services.

Parents

I wrote this poem after two weeks of being in an inclusive community where gifts and differences were valued. When I first met my daughter after this experience I was struck by how differently I experienced her.

Saturday Morning 7/17/93

I looked into Annie's Eyes this morning-
In this morning I looked into Annie's eyes.
My daughter's eyes.
I searched for what was wrong. What is her disability?
As I looked into her eyes, at her hair blown by nights tossing and turning,
she smiled and smiled. My heart hurt with sensations all over.
Where is it?
I could find no wrong with Annie in her beauty playing with her dog this morning.

Polly danced and barked. Annie sprayed water at Polly's barks.
They danced round the room.

I felt like I was coming through a thick fog this morning.

I cannot see anything wrong with Annie.
I cannot feel anywhere in my body that tight almost nauseous
feeling I always have when I think I have seen what's wrong with
Annie.
In this morning my body feels no tightness, no nausea as I look,
and look at Annie.
She is simply a beautiful, joy filled child having morning spraying
love and water
at her barking dog, Polly.

I sit this morning   feeling a trembling in my belly.
How precious is this moment of me seeing Annie as she is.

I am angry for all the labellers who have sought to steal
my daughter's life.

I am sad that I have so many times taken their lies inside me
seeing Annie as retarded or organic brain damaged or disabled or
whatever.
I have often seen my child with eyes of guilt and shame.
I have been robbed of the present.

It is so obvious at this moment that there are only children.
People filled with gifts and possibilities.

I feel my belly calm, warm, my heart trembling, my eyes with
tears, my smile soft.
I see Annie so clearly this moment of dog spraying laughter.

I know I do not have to live the Labellers lie.
I know in this morning the truth.

Mike Green.[1]

Parents of disabled children have become revolutionaries by the simple act of refusing to stop valuing their children. The current world-view of disabled children, particularly those who have very significant impairments, is so negative that the birth of such a child is usually thought of as a tragedy to be avoided at almost any cost. If such a child does survive then parents are subjected to an onslaught of professional interventions which , in the past aimed at separation and isolation of the child in institutions, and now more commonly try to turn the parents into teacher/therapists at home. Their children are declared defective, and from this position society struggles to see their life as anything else but sad and hopeless, unless medicine finds a cure.

Under the influence of this world-view many parents have given away their children to residential hospitals or 'schools', or thrown themselves into organising therapies, fund-raising for medical research, campaigning for specialist and separate provision, and setting up impairment-specific charities and support groups.

Yet, a few parents have not shared this worldview. The relationship with the child profoundly challenged their preconceptions to such a point that a monumental leap was made in allegiance from conventional society to their child. They held onto their unconditional love and instead went to 'war' with the world:

When I first had Kim he was my son.

A year later he was epileptic and developmentally delayed. At eighteen months he had special needs and he was a special child. He had a mild to moderate learning difficulty. He was mentally handicapped. I was told not to think about his future.

I struggled with all this.

By the time he was four he had special educational needs. He was a statemented child. He was dyspraxic, epileptic, developmentally delayed and he had complex communication problems.

Two years later, aged six, he was severely epileptic (EP), cerebral palsied (CP) and had complex learning difficulties.

At eight he had severe intractable epilepsy with associated communication problems. He was showing a marked developmental regression. He had severe learning difficulties.

At nine he came out of segregated schooling and he slowly became my son again. Never again will he be anything else but Kim - a son, a brother, a friend, a pupil, a teacher, a person.

Pippa Murray - Let our Children Be.[2]

These parents redefined their job description. They no longer saw their primary role as people who could help their child to become less of a problem to society, but helping society to become less of a problem to their child. Society has not always welcomed this approach - in fact the struggle undertaken by parents has brought out into the open the unconscious motives of a system which purports to be there to protect the needs of the weak and vulnerable, but in fact protects the needs of the strong and greedy.

Truth is often the hardest fact of life to face and to come to terms with, our children live the reality of this world 'imposed upon them', they lose their innocence quicker than most, because they have to struggle and battle with it as individuals every day of their lives, 'out there', because as parents we have no rights, we have no authority or control. Decisions are taken out of our hands and 'they' wreak havoc with the lives of our children. I feel as powerless as a child because whatever I say is ignored, professionals refuse to accept what I say as valid or important, then I am forced to witness their crimes against my child and suffer it as a parent without power, without control and without a say

Anna Jeronymedes (*from a letter to the author)*

In many countries of the 'developed' world these parents came up against the systematic exclusion of their children from mainstream schools and communities. This is reinforced by laws and practices which deny them the choice of supporting their children to be living a valued life in the community. Consequently, many parents have been identified with high profile battles with educational professionals and legal structures, which still have the power to compel their children into, segregated provision. Most of these parents are very 'ordinary' people who would never have thought of themselves as revolutionaries or human rights activists, and their courage has been tested to the limits by the strength of resistance of the authorities concerned. Their often desperate need for advice and support has led them to seek out other like-minded people. They have acted as catalysts, bringing their passion, anger and urgency into the public arena.

Disabled People

Living on the margin either burns you out and kills you, or it turns you into a dreamer, someone who really knows what sort of change will help and who can just about taste it; someone who is prepared to do anything to bring about change. If these dreamers are liberated, if they are brought back into the arms of society, they become the architects of a new community; a community that has the capacity to support everyone's needs and interactions.

Judith Snow - Bradwin Address 1988

Disabled people, the excluded, have always struggled to break free from the limitations others put on our lives. Up until the recent time this has usually been an isolated struggle by individuals trying to prove society wrong about them. This has led many disabled people to attempt to function within the able-bodied world, achieving able-bodied things without the help that we need and with a smile on our face. This has been to counteract the assumptions that we are incapable, dependent, bitter and twisted. However, whilst doing it we were always aware that only some of us could take this path whilst our more 'severely impaired' brothers and sisters were doomed to live a wasted, hidden, institutionalised life.

However, on the backs of these many individual challenges to the common world view of us as 'useless', society inched forwards to a time when it has been possible for us to organise ourselves into a collective movement for civil rights. Like parents, the common goal, which brought us together, was to turn people's attention away from our individual impairments and on to the environment in which we have to live. Our perspective we encapsulated as the Social Model of Disability. We compared this to the current understanding and practices around us which we named as the Medical Model of Disability, and which inevitably lead to our exclusion. Because it is a fight for personal survival as well as a political movement there is no possibility that disabled people will ever give up until we have achieved our ends.

The chance to support our youngest members through campaigning alongside parents has empowered us, and in return we have given a useful analysis to the struggle, tools to help re-think the situation, and role-models for other disabled people including children.

Young People

Sometimes it seems that most adults think it is okay to guess what young people want. Others don't bother about young people's views at all. This happens in all walks of life - young people in care, school children, young disabled people or those who have got themselves involved in the courts. Some adults think that they can represent young people's views. In the UK for example, we are not allowed to vote until we are eighteen years old. We cannot become members of parliament until we reach twenty-one. Professionals and people who work with young people should listen to us and work with us as individuals instead of thinking they know better.

Everybody needs to have a say. Having the opportunity to express views is the way a person learns to communicate. By having those views taken seriously, a person learns self-respect and how to respect others. Young people of today are the future and we believe we have the right - and need the chance - to shape our futures.

All young people have the right to make decisions about our lives, whether it is something simple like what to wear in the morning, or something more important like who to live with if our parents divorce. This is not to say that young people should make final decisions about everything, but it is important that we get a say and that our opinions are taken seriously.

It is important to listen to all young people, especially those with emotional, behavioural or learning difficulties. These young people are often forgotten because communicating with them is a challenge. Everybody needs to be listened to. Everyone has the right to a voice. Often it is seen as a privilege to have a life where we can make our own choices. But it is more than that - it is a basic human right.

Lucy Mason and Lizzie Kenyon 1999
(UNICEF magazine article for Article 12)

Young people were not organised until very recently in conventional ways, but nevertheless have a strong culture of resistance to adult mistreatment. Unfortunately most of this resistance is seen in negative terms, the label 'Challenging Behaviour' or 'Behavioural Difficulties' illustrating the professional response to children who do not, or cannot do what is being asked of them. It does not question whether what is being asked of them is appropriate for those children.

For many young people the only ways to protest about anything is to take a path of non-co-operation, pretty well guaranteed to bring forth a negative response from those who are being defied. Sometimes though, people do ask the question 'Is this child trying to say something to which we should be listening', and when they do, learning and growth can take place. Some exceptional adults have gone further, and handed back some control to young people with an expectation that given information and responsibility, young people can create new solutions to problems which have baffled past generations.

I'm not sure that calling in outside experts does much good. You already have scores of experts in the school - the children. They know what's going wrong and lots of ways to make things better. The children help us run our school. They work with us and not against us. That happens when the staff know that the children want to learn and succeed. They have plenty of good ideas. They always have a huge impact on their school - for better or worse. You often find that the worst bullies turn out to be the best leaders.

For just a very few children, all these ways don't work. They would be excluded if they were at other schools. But we think exclusion wouldn't help that child learn to solve their problems. When a few children keep behaving badly, they only get away with it because the rest of the class lets them. This is partly because the 'bad' ones refuse to accept some things which the 'good' ones also think are wrong or unfair. Excluding the worst ones is not the answer. A few more will take their place. You can only really change the difficult children if you work in three ways:

help them learn how to change their behaviour;

listen to the class and work with them to make changes that they choose;

and work with the whole school using their ideas on how to make the school a fairer, safer, easier place for everyone to work in.

Classteacher - Highfield Junior School, Plymouth [3]

In particular it has been noticed that young people, until mistaught by adults, are natural inclusionists, and therefore have been brought into the heart of changing practice, particularly within schools. It can be said that these young people are modelling a possible future for us all.

The growing awareness in society that young people should have a say in matters which concern them, has been reflected in the Children Act which requires adults to take notice of the 'Ascertainable wishes of the child', but it has been noted that this often does not happen.

In 1996 the first national organisation run by and for young people was launched. It is called Article 12 and is based on the UN Convention on the Rights of the Child. At around the same time a group of young disabled and non-disabled people set up a steering committee to help them develop a national campaigning group called 'Young Pioneers (now called 'Young and Powerful'). Together with 'Children's Express', a young peoples' news agency, there is the beginning of an organised, representative voice for young people.

Professionals

First we built institutions with high walls, then institutions with low walls, and now we can build institutions with no walls at all

John McKnight

It is the role of the professional which is perhaps the most surprising in bringing about change. Self-interest more obviously plays a part at least in the three previous groups desire for change, but for professionals inclusion has often meant the most painful re-evaluation of the work that they have done with implications that have appeared to be the opposite of self-interest, more akin to professional suicide!

Some individual service providers began to see, often to their dismay, that everything they had been trying to do, despite their good intentions, was not working. Not only was it not working, but was actually creating the very problem it was trying to solve. Many of these were working in the field of adults with 'learning difficulties' who had enthusiastically redesigned now outdated residential provision for their clients into 'community based' services such as Group Homes and "Care in the Community'.

The shocking fact was that even though their clients were now living in ordinary houses, in ordinary streets, doing much more ordinary things, many of them still had no-one in their life who wasn't paid to be there - . They realised that the existence of services could prevent and replace real caring relationships from developing naturally within communities, and this was impoverishing both their clients, and the communities. The question they then had to ask was *how could they use their resources to support people with significant physical, intellectual or emotional impairments to build real relationships within their own communities?*. The result of asking this question has been the development of many experimental tools, techniques and projects, including the closing down of Special Schools, Adult Training Centres and Sheltered Workshops and the transference of the resources thus released into inclusive mainstream schools and colleges, Supported Living and Employment schemes, the concept of 'Person-Centred Planning', and voluntary circles of support.

The early professional pioneers of this change of focus had recognised something about themselves - that the 'medical model' has many failures to which society responds with an organisational floor-brush, sweeping them out of sight into institutions, hospitals and prisons- and this acceptance of failure is hurtful to the humanity of everyone engaged in the process. It is hurtful because it makes us all feel limited and defeated, and implies that we can never learn how to help some people.

The involvement of professionals in the inclusion movement is, in reality, very understandable when seen as their human desire to not accept false limitations on their ability to learn and solve problems. Yet this stance is very challenging to nearly all current policy and practice and for some professionals it has meant losing their career, their salary and their status within the Special Needs World - yet they have done it. Most have gone on to develop a new career in the promotion of inclusion, but their courage and integrity must not be underestimated. In the end it is only when professionals decide to change their practice that inclusion can become a reality.

It is the coming together of these four key groups of people that has created the Inclusion Movement.

On the journey of course, we are gathering many other fellow travellers, because the philosophy of inclusion has great appeal to many people who long themselves to live and be part of human communities which support and nurture the soul, and in which we can all feel safe to grow old.

The Social Model of Disability

Revolutions begin when people who are defined as problems achieve the power to redefine the problem

John McKnight – The Careless Society

The social model came from disabled people and our realisation that the suffering associated with being a disabled person comes almost entirely from other people and they way they have responded to our existence. Our impairments may, or may not bring inherent difficulties such as pain, but these are trivial in comparison to the devastation caused by the onslaught of the medical model described above. Because most of us are not ill at all, but have injuries or genetic conditions of a permanent nature, the goal of 'getting better' is impossible to achieve, but to change the way we are treated as disabled people is possible. Therefore, the social model is full of hope for us.

The Birth of a Movement

Disabled people realised that we had to take the initiative if things were to change. We decided to give up the role of 'patient' and become activists instead.

In Britain, a resident in Le Court, a Cheshire Home for physically disabled people, became one of the first political leaders of disabled people. In 1966 he wrote one of the first books written by disabled people about disability issues (Stigma by Paul Hunt, Geoffrey Chapman, London,) and organised some of the first examples of direct action including Le Courts Residents strikes and management take-overs. In 1972 he wrote a letter the Guardian Newspaper:

> *Severely physically handicapped people find themselves in isolated, unsuitable institutions, where their views are ignored and they are subject to authoritarian and often cruel regimes. I am proposing the formation of a consumer group to put forward nationally the views of actual and potential residents of these successors to the workhouse*

Paul Hunt, the Guardian 20th September 1972.

Many disabled people responded to Paul's' rally, and some formed The Union of The Physically Impaired Against Segregation. This group became, in effect, a 'think tank', operating primarily through a confidential, internal circular made necessary by the vulnerable situation of most of its members living within residential institutions. The social model of disability came from the minds of these people although their organisation did not itself manage to attract the mass membership required to bring about the changes they sought. The organisation was, however, one of the first to adopt a policy statement and a constitution which exacted an internal discipline and the possibility of a democratic, representative structure. This helped create an impetus to many other small groups of disabled people forming campaigns and coalitions, themselves inspired by the Independent Living Movement in the USA. Members of UPIAS, recognising that they were not a representative national organisation, called together a Steering Committee from amongst all these organisations. This was the origin of The British Council of Organisations of Disabled People (BCODP).

To belong to this body you had to be an organisation <u>of</u> disabled people. 'Of' meant that the decision-making body - it's management committee or council, had to have a majority of disabled people with the power to vote (51% or more). That was the only rule. Groups which were campaigns, support groups, arts groups, coalitions and Centres for Independent Living, as well as impairment specific organisations, such as the British Deaf Association or the Spinal Injuries Association, were all welcome to join as long as they were controlled by the membership. Together we have struggled to design policies upon which there is widespread agreement amongst the membership, and to promote those policies, rather than individual viewpoints, when we are asked to speak on behalf of Disabled people. It has been this ability to speak with a united voice which is finally moving us (in Britain) towards true citizenship through enforceable civil rights and a transfer of resources from medical model provision to provision based on the social model of disability.

In the same year, 1980, a new international organisation of disabled people was formed :

*The Disabled Peoples International (DPI) emerged in the same year as the BCODP out of the anger of 200 disabled delegates at a two-and-a-half-thousand strong Rehabilitation International conference in Winnipeg. Disabled delegates were enraged at the decision not to ensure disabled people's representation on the International Year of Disabled People's organising committee. In protest they walked out, and the now director of DPI, Henry Enns, addressed the boycott of **disabled** people who came from over thirty countries, saying "Do I hear you want to form your own International Organisation of Disabled People?" There was a resounding 'Yes!' to this question without a single dissension. He then called upon delegates to go back to their respective countries and start a national assembly of disabled people that could feed into an international body.*

Jane Campbell and Mike Oliver – Disability Politics.[4]

The excitement and energy created by the formation of DPI added to the sense of 'uprising ' which was spreading amongst disabled people in many countries of the world, including our own.

Defining the Problem

We thought we needed to define the nature of the problem we wanted solved instead of the fruitless search for medical cures. We thought it important therefore to use language to clearly separate our personal 'condition' or 'impairment' from the response to it. This definition of disabled people came about early in 1997. It has developed in consultation with disabled people and their organisations around the country:

IMPAIRMENT is a characteristic, feature or attribute within an individual which is long term and may or may not be the result of disease, injury or congenital condition and may:

1. affect that individual's appearance in a way which is not acceptable to society and / or

2. affect the functioning of that individual's mind or body either because of, or regardless of, society and/or

3. also cause pain, fatigue, affect communication, memory and/ or reduced consciousness. DISABILITY is the disadvantage or restriction of activity caused by the systems and practices in society, which excludes people who have impairments.

(Therefore disability, like racism or sexism, is discrimination and social oppression).

DISABLED PEOPLE are those people with impairments who are disabled by barriers in society. This includes people with physical impairments, people with visual impairments, people with learning difficulties, deaf people, people who are hard of hearing and people who have or have experienced mental illness / distress.

BCODP with its comparatively clear analysis, was influential at the inaugural meeting of 'Disabled People's International' (Singapore 1981) where these definitions were officially adopted by the disabled community. We thereafter called ourselves 'Disabled People', meaning victims of a social oppression. It was our politicisation.

Rejecting Labels - Reclaiming Identity

We will be the labels they have given us. When they look at us they see the label. They do not see children who one day will be mothers or fathers, be bakers or carpenters, shop workers or office workers, artists or mountaineers, poets or politicians. This means that people with learning difficulties will leave school with no qualifications, unable to face any job interview, and with little or no idea of what they would like to do. It is not surprising that people with learning difficulties end up unemployed or in work experience or adult training centres for the rest of their lives.

Special Schools – And Now We Are Different, People First - Scotland.

We rejected the term 'Handicapped' as it implies limits which we do not accept are real, and which puts the problem of disability back onto the individual.

The term 'Mentally Handicapped" was felt to be particularly offensive, and people with this label chose the definition for themselves as 'People with Learning Difficulties". Difficulties, not disabilities, because difficulties can be overcome with the right support. In the choosing of the name this group of people were also rejecting the notion that they were forever limited by the nature of their impairment. It was said that the labels put on them were part of the 'veil' of the medical model which obscured their individuality and potential:

Regaining Self-Respect

I saw few images of disability. Those that existed made a strong impression on me, strengthening my resolve that at all costs I would not be like 'them'. Charity posters (like Mencap's 'little Stephen' with tear rolling down cheek, or the kid with muscular dystrophy abandoned with wheelchair in the centre of wasteland),Badges of Fortitude in the Girl Guides, or Children of Courage on the TV, 'Treasure Island' and'Heidi' with Captain Hook and Little Clara, prayers to heal the sick in assembly (and to give thanks that there but for the grace....), International Years and flag days - all led me to the same reaction: "I'm not like that.

Faced with the able-bodied images it seemed vastly preferable to conform (however inadequately) to the demands of able-bodiedness. I consistently and emphatically rejected any attempts to describe me as disabled, preferring to continue struggling - quietly.

It was fortuitous that my work interests lay in the field of disability. (Rejecting images of disability, however forcefully, did not prevent me from wanting to become involved with disabled people, though firmly in a 'helping' role -(was this me desperately staving off further attempts at labelling?) If my interests had been otherwise, I might never have attended the conference organised by my college community action group. Organised by non-disabled people (how many disabled people do you find in higher education?), two disabled women were amongst the invited workshop leaders, lending an air of credibility to the proceedings.

Joining their session 'Politics of Disability', it was like a dam burst. Here were two women who identified themselves willingly as Disabled! Here were two women, Disabled and strong. They were unlike all the images fed to me by the able-bodied world. For the first time, I realised that in trying to determine my identity, I had only ever been presented with able-bodied conceptions of able-bodiedness and disability. At last I realised that other definitions could exist. Like those two disabled women, I could find my self, and my self did not have to exist on able-bodied terms!

Liz Crow [5]

We realised that we had absorbed a large part of societies negative view of us and believed it to be true, which had in turn allowed us to accept our mistreatment without much protest. It put us off wanting to organise our own movement because we didn't really want to be seen with other people 'like us'. This 'internalised oppression' had to be challenged amongst ourselves. We had to discard feelings of shame and worthlessness about ourselves and each other, replacing them with a positive identity and pride in who we really were. Only when we have achieved true equality will we be able to throw away this identity and just be people.

Rights not Charity

Our needs ands related provision have been always been defined by non-disabled people, and non-disabled people are the providers, the funders and the judges of its success. Governments have therefore seen our 'rights' as rights to special provision and services', and have handed much of the role of provider over to charities, most of which are controlled by non-disabled people.

However, what we want is the right participate in ordinary life with the support we need to do so - self-advocacy, access, interpretation, user-led personal assistance, inclusive education, anti-discrimination legislation. Specialist services can become barriers to this goal.

Charities are still reliant on public donations and therefore a positive public perception of the things they provide has to be created. Some charities have budgets of millions of pounds and consequently have the economic power to market themselves - a power which disabled people, poor people, young people are denied. Charity images rely on invoking pity and fear and therefore carry a huge responsibility for the climate in which we all live.

Self-Representation

We are full time, unpaid researchers of our own conditions and destiny. Under the paving stone lay the grass, as the saying went, and under the layers of ostracisation and stereotyping and bigotry, under the buy-your-distance bleeding-heart charity culture, under the 'victim', 'brave', 'sufferer' crippled terminology, is the beginning of our own definition of ourselves and a constructive relationship with our conditions and disabilities on our own terms.

David Hevey [6]

We realised that in order to remove the 'veil' of the medical model, we had to make direct contact with people so they could know us and what we thought, and in order to do this we have to develop means of self-representation. This meant setting up our own organisations, writing our own books, running our own training courses, singing our own songs, speaking up in meetings and at conferences, refusing to shut up.

The Myth of Independence

When I first left home and moved into living 'independently' in my own little flat, I was extremely proud of the fact that I did not need a Home Help. I discovered that if I shortened the length of the vacuum cleaner hose by removing most of the metal bits, I could crawl around the floor vacuuming. I also discovered that I could wash my sheets by hand in the bath, and that if I never bought heavy tins and jars of things at the same time as potatoes, I could just about carry all my shopping home myself. People conveyed to me their admiration at my 'fierce independence' and thought that I would be insulted if they offered to do any of these things for me. No one noticed (including me) that it took most of my time and energy to do the things which took others about one tenth of the effort.

Gradually however, as I got drawn into the world and all its interesting possibilities, I began to realise that I would have to make some choices about where to expend my time and energy. Would it be better to paint and sell pictures, or chair a local 'self-help' group of disabled people than crawl around the floor with a vacuum cleaner. I decided eventually that although I could be self-sufficient in my daily living chores, it made more sense to develop my skills and make a real contribution to my community, and to ask for a Home Help.

A few years later my horizons had grown to such an extent that I decided to ask my friends if they would support me to undertake something which I could not possibly contemplate without their help - keeping my baby. Such was the quality of my relationships that I had a whole team of volunteers who offered practical and emotional support to both myself and my daughter. I now had a Home Help and a Circle of Support upon whom I depended.

More years went past and I started to dream about the kind of world in which I wished my daughter to grow up, recognising the enormous task there was ahead to make this dream a reality. I reached out to other parents, to disabled people, my circle of support and complete strangers in order to create an organisation from which we could all campaign for, and promote inclusion. I now have a Home Help, a Circle of Support, funders, a full-time paid assistant, a management committee, an office, an adapted van with lift, and a membership base of hundreds of like-minded people connected to others all over the world. My list of people upon whom I depend (and who depend on me) has expanded enormously as has my ability to make my unique contribution to the world, and to help others to make theirs.

During this period of my life, my physical impairment has got worse. I now use a power wheelchair to go out when once I could walk a fair distance on crutches, and I no longer have the stamina for the all-night debates in which I used to engage, yet in our new 'social model' definition, I am still 'fiercely independent.' because I have not lost any control over my life.

It has been assumed that all disabled people want to be independent as possible, and few would question this. It is part of western culture to see the need for help from others as a bad thing. All children are encouraged to leave behind signs of their dependence - breasts, nappies, bottles as soon as possible. This continues into all aspects of 'growing-up' - learning to feed oneself, dress oneself, bath oneself, even amuse oneself. These are all considered to be signs of maturity and worthy of applause. Wanting 'attention' is considered a punishable offence from the age of about two onwards. It is not surprising then that this value judgement is extended into other areas of life until it becomes difficult for most people to admit that they need help, or cannot manage alone. Loneliness and isolation are painfully common, but the connection between 'independence' and aloneness is seldom made. Yet independence is a complete illusion even for the most able human being.

People in the western world are expected to live within boundaries set by what they can manage more-or-less on their own (unless they can pay for assistance). They agree to this because they are persuaded that it is demeaning to do anything else. For 'average', non-disabled people, these limits are usually wide enough to live an acceptable life, because the scope built into the services and systems available to the general population, enable such lives to be created. The whole point about being dis-abled is that these structures exclude people who are not 'average'. Disabled people can only be en-abled by altering the structures and systems, or providing individualised assistance from other people.

By the simple act of saying "I need your help to do this thing that I want to do", we are able to break free from these limits imposed by isolation, and can begin to see that in fact, with co-operation and team work, human beings have limits only caused by a lack of imagination, or courage to dream.

Essentially we are social beings who live inter-dependently. The goal of independence can therefore be misused as a prison for disabled people. It often carries with it an implied assumption of which disabled people are painfully aware, that there will not be human beings in the disabled persons life who freely want to be with them, and help them achieve their goals. They must learn to manage as best they can and be as little trouble as possible to others. This explains why so many classes in 'special schools, colleges and training centres seem to be obsessed with sandwich making and bed making, rather than sex-education or any form of academic or vocational learning.

Independence Through User-Led Services

We knew that we had to regain control over our own lives even when we need help from others to function. Unless we do this, we can never make a real contribution to society because our own thoughts will never be expressed through our actions, only those of other people, our 'carers'. Having no control over your life also makes you totally vulnerable to abuse, the evidence of which is all around us. Therefore we redefined 'independence' to mean having control over your life, not 'doing things without help'.

Disabled people and people with learning difficulties are challenging this whole concept of independence by defining independence as being in control of their own lives, including the level and type of support they need. Clearly it is about building peer relationships rather than learning to live without them.

The Independent Living Movement is our response to the over-professionalising of services which put the power in the hands of the providers. It is about defining our own needs, employing our own assistants, living in our own homes, pursuing our own goals, being responsible for our own lives .

Assistants not 'Carers'

MOTHER-CARE
don't call me her carer
it smells of something worse
of the twisted professions
Mother – Care
still misusing this word
with a meaning quite different
to what caring is in truth
and unfulfilled people
gaining power and loot
the career following, cupboard loving
paid pretend friends
and employed nurturers
who need crips to depend

I am her MOTHER
Her full time adorer
Who explodes when she smiles
Whose heart breaks when she cries
Who worries constantly
And continually sheds
The tears which cushion her
Ride through this mess
I'm here because I love her
How about you?
Don't compare my contribution
To what you do.
   Clair Lewis © 1999 [7]

Personal Assistants (called Attendants in the USA) are not 'carers', and nor are advocates or support workers. The term 'carer' applied to a professional relationship, has no place in the social model of disability. It simply confuses to use a word that implies an emotional relationship instead of one which is practical. It gives the impression that needs are being met which are not being met, and could never be met, by a paid worker. Carers are the people who care about us, our friends, family, colleagues at work, not the people who deliver our meals-on-wheels. (Some paid people do cross the line and become part of our social circle, but this is an *additional relationship*, independent of the role)

Young Carers

The growth of the 'Young Carers' association is evidence of how deeply confused society can be. When a disabled person chooses to live and 'ordinary' life in the community, we do it for the most part without anything like adequate support, in an inaccessible environment and often in the face of unhelpful or hostile attitudes. It sometimes happens then that our children, who love us, try and fill some of the unmet needs by providing some personal assistance. This *should never be necessary*, and would not be necessary if disabled people had access to the resources we need to live 'independently'. However, because society cannot grasp the fact that many of us are in 'caring' roles, they try instead to support the young person, actually by exploiting them and patting them on the back at the same time. It also degrades the parent instead of valuing her or him.

Support Not Respite

The concept of 'respite care' also belongs in the mistaken ideology of the medical model. It is fundamentally insulting to disabled people, including children, and yet another example of viewing disabled people as a burden to the able-bodied rather than a group of people who are being denied the support we need. The fact that a good number of young people seem to enjoy attending 'respite care' centres should not be seen as evidence that they are the right thing to do. (Many of these young people see them as places to get 'respite from their carers'!) but all it shows is the lack of choice in their lives.

The problem which drives people to create these sticking-plaster services is that too much 'caring' is done by too few people - the isolation of families, the existence of segregated schools, the inaccessibility of mainstream services, and the lack of caring communities - these are the real problems. As communities disappear, and all adults are needing to earn a living, the problem of caring for all children is becoming apparent. This is resulting in increased reliance on after-school clubs, childminders and holiday playschemes or camps, but no one would contemplate calling them 'respite care' for non-disabled children.

Disabled People an Asset

The insidious nature of the medical model with its eugenic undertones, has affected the worlds perception of disabled people so profoundly that our huge contribution to the quality of life is invisible to most people. The countless personal relationships which we have forged with those around us, despite their fear, the creativity of our artists, writers, poets and musicians, our humour and empathy, our ingenuity and flexibility, our courage and generosity of spirit - all have been overlooked whilst society had fixed its gaze on our 'needs'. People have not recognised our moderating role in society, created by our very inability to conform to inhuman pressures of speed or appearance. People do not consciously understand that impairment is part of the human experience, not exclusive to specific kinds of people, and without our constant modelling of the power of the human spirit to adapt to and transcend such experiences, life would feel much more frightening than it does. Only a few understand that it is our ability to adapt and transcend which is really worth studying, not our limitations, because this is what throws light on our human nature. Furthermore, our own thoughts insights, initiatives and collective political struggles are unreported, dismissed or attributed to our non-disabled 'carers' or professionals we have influenced. Our heroes and heroines go unsung, except by each other, though many of us have lived and died tirelessly working to make the world a better place.

TO OUR WARRIORS

We have our warriors
Battling with society
And disease.
We carry our scars
On our bodies
And in our hearts.
The deepest hurts are when we turn
The knives of the oppressor
Against each other.

We lose too many of our warriors too soon.
With too many years unlived,
Too many battles unwon.
And yet each one's fight
Moves us all forward.
Brings closer the day when
The doors of all the day centres, homes, hostels,
Special thises and that's
Will clatter empty in the wind.
The day when we all will be free.

So rest easy my sisters and brothers.
Lie peaceful in the earth
Or scattered in the air.
Your rage on earth blew up a storm
We will inherit your thunder, your lightening,
Your love.
We will fight on

Sue Napolitano[8]

Many people, for example, know the story of Helen Keller and how she learnt to communicate with hearing people through the use of touch, but how many of you know what she did when she grew up? Braille was invented by a blind teenager, but at the time he was told that he was performing tricks to pretend that blind people could read, which everyone ' knew' was impossible. Louis Braille never knew that a hundred years later all blind young people would have the chance of an education - because of him.

Most of the real changes which have liberated disabled people from ineffective, institutionalised lives, have been brought about by our own efforts, with just a few allies.

One story which illustrates the nature of the struggle is that of Anne McDonald and Rosemary Crossley, made public through their book 'Annie's Coming Out". Anne McDonald is an Australian, institutionalised as a baby because she had cerebral palsy. She could not speak and it was therefore assumed that she could not think. She was left to lie all day on a mat on the floor, gradually 'bowing' due to spasms of the spinal muscles.

Her 'prognosis' was an early death due to breathing difficulties which, the experts said, would inevitably occur as the curvature increased. Rosemary Crossley was a play therapist, employed to occupy the more able of the children in the institution.

Rosemary had enough attention to notice 'something' in Anne's eyes which led her to believe that Annie was a thinking person locked inside a body which she could not control. Together, she and Annie discovered that by Rosemary physically restraining some of Annie's unwanted 'large' movements, she could intentionally point to symbols on a board. This enabled Annie, for the first tie in her life, to make a choice. These symbols were eventually developed into letters whereupon Annie demonstrated that she knew how to read (by watching Sesame Street on the ward television). Thus Annie began to speak.

She had a great deal to say, including the fact that she wished to leave the hated institution. No one in authority would countenance this, arguing that Annie was 'severely retarded', could nor make an informed choice, and was being manipulated by her therapist, Rosemary.

Rosemary was suspended from her job and suffered may attacks on her integrity, and much abandonment by her co-workers, including those who agreed with her in private.

At the age of eighteen, Annie took the institution to court where she managed to persuade the Judge that she was speaking for herself and was therefore entitled to choose to leave the hospital. She won her case and left to live with Rosemary. She eventually went to university and wrote the book in order to spread the technique of 'Facilitated Communication' all around the world, giving many 'silenced' people a voice. Equally important, she has forced everyone who knows of her to consider the possibility that there is a whole, thinking, feeling person locked inside every living person however appearances may suggest otherwise. Most recently this has been re-inforced by stories of people coming out of what had been called 'persistent vegetative states' after years, and beginning to communicate again.

Disabled People are Carers

From the point of view of the medical model, this is almost a contradiction in terms. I remember growing up and not once seeing an image, reading a story, or ever being told about a disabled person who was a parent. The possibility of my having children was not mentioned and in such a climate, I did not broach the subject myself. Nor do I remember disabled people being portrayed as friends, lovers, or givers of any kind. I do remember some stories of disabled people achieving independence Against the Odds - who could forget the endless showings of 'Reach for the Sky' the heroic story of Douglas Bader, an airforce pilot shot down during the war, who bravely learnt to walk unaided after losing both his legs, and went on to return to his former glory, shooting the enemy from his fighter aeroplane. It did not inspire me very much. Where were the role models I could follow and admire, who were needed and loved by people other than their parents? Nowhere to be seen.

I now realise as an adult who happens to know lots of disabled people that we are all those things, including parents. I am one myself, and many people love me and depend on me for all sorts of things, but this reality of our lives is made invisible and without any support structures in place. Oh, there is the child protection team hovering in the background, ready to swoop down and 'save' our children from our 'inadequate' parenting, but no recognition that with a little extra resources and consideration it would be a much easier job.

The difficulty in recognising disabled people as 'givers' is a legacy of our 'worthless' status in the past. There are hopeful signs however that this is beginning to change. Despite a great deal of initial resistance, many teachers in schools which have included disabled young people have said that, in practice, the child had given more to the school than the school had given to the child:

I have been Kitty's teacher for nearly four years now and together with my religious studies class she's learned lots about the different religions of the world and how people feel about their beliefs. However, it is not just Kitty who has been a student in my class. Over the years I have learned so many things from her example.

These are just a few of them:

I've always been committed to the idea of equal opportunities but I've learned that there are no limits to the concept of inclusivity.

I've learned the value of determination from Kitty, her Mum and whole family, as without this Kitty would not be in my GCSE class today.

I've learned the positive value for other students of having the privilege of Kitty in their class. Students have learned that different needs are just that - different - and are able to be taken in your stride alongside every other different need of each individual student in the class.

I've seen the joy of friendship when Kitty's classmates make notes for her when she's not been present, without being asked, because they know it will help their friend when she gets back.

I've taken pride in the sensitive way children can treat each other as she is helped by others in the classroom.

I've learned to challenge other people's assumptions, along with my own. When Kitty scored the second highest mark in a test, it was to her that others turned for help, and this has continued. If you don't know - ask Kitty.

I've learned that just because an issue isn't mine personally, it doesn't mean it's got nothing to do with me.

I've listened carefully, as although Kitty is softly spoken, it doesn't mean she has nothing to say - and she tells really bad jokes!

Having Kitty in my class has been such a positive experience for me, for her fellow classmates as well as for Kitty herself. I don't think I've ever been prouder of students than when Kitty won a school award for achievement in my subject. She walked onto the platform alongside the other award winners and received her trophy proudly, and as she came down the stairs the student in front of her, without thinking - turned to help her friend down the stairs. This scene sums up some of the most beneficial aspects of inclusive education aiming for an inclusive society.

Cath Brookes about Kitty Gilbert, a pupil with the

Down's Syndrome label. [9]

Person Centred Planning (The Inside-Out Approach)

The medical model usually starts from a position of trying to fit people into already existing services. Person-centred planning starts from a very different place. The early pioneers were providers of adult services for people with 'severe' learning difficulties and/or challenging behaviour - the people everyone had deemed hopeless.

Micheline

They started by discovering the interests and skills of the person, and then worked towards opening up 'community spaces' in which the person would be welcome to develop these skills and interests. Person-centred planning is based on notions of 'listening' and 'dreaming'. People who engage in person-centred planning see themselves as 'servants' not 'managers', empowering rather than controlling their clients. They do not see their goal as training their clients to do without help, but to discover the rightful limits of paid service providers within healthy, caring communities. They also saw their role as akin to anthropology, trying to learn about a group of people who had been abandoned and ignored by society, forced to live a separate life, and also to study themselves - the perpetrators - as they struggled to change the way they worked. It is a deeply thoughtful approach.

The early practitioners grew to include educators who saw prevention of isolation being a better option than attempting to re-integrate adults into a world in which they were uninvited strangers.

The Magical Power of Attention

Listening
If you are going to work with me,
You have to listen to me.
And you can't just listen with your ears,
Because it will go to your head too fast
If you listen slow,
with your whole body,
some of what I say
will enter your heart.

Christine Mayer 'Celebrating the Ordinary' [10]

If you think about it, real attention is what everyone is looking for. Most conversations are not really two-way forms of communication, but rather two intermittent monologues, each person trying to get the other to listen to them. I have been very fortunate in my life because in my early twenties, I met someone who taught me that it is possible to "get" attention by taking turns. When I discovered the art of splitting time in half and sharing it equally between myself and another person, I then became aware of the magical power of attention.

When people really listen to me I can remember things I thought I had forgotten. When people can allow me to feel the feelings that go with my past, I can untangle them from present time situations, and think about things more rationally. When I really listen to other people, I can see the difference between their "hurt" and their real selves, and sometimes I can provide them with an opportunity to do their own untangling. We seem to be born to use each other in this way.

An Explanation of Irrationality

Attention allows us to heal ourselves emotionally of past hurts.

In Seattle in the USA, about forty years ago, a man called Harvey Jackins deduced from careful observation an idea which will, in the fullness of time, revolutionise our understanding of human intelligence. The idea is that emotional distress reduces our ability to think rationally until our innate healing process is enabled to operate. The healing process is physiological, involving both mind and body – the mind recalls the original distress and the body automatically engages upon a physical process made visible through tears, laughter, shaking, sweating, yawning and non-repetitive talking. The only requirement for this process is the non-judgemental attention of someone else. Every newborn baby is equipped with this self-healing mechanism. Luckily, most mothers are 'programmed' to provide the partnership. When the process is allowed to be completed, hurtful experiences become no more than memories from which we can learn.

However, in the more usual circumstance when the process is interrupted or thwarted, the mind is left with unprocessed information and a compulsion to search for the attention to finish the process. It is these accumulations of unprocessed information, often including powerful emotions, which leads to pockets of irrationality in all of our thinking. It could be said that all of the worlds problems could be easily solved were it not for the effect of past distress on the human intelligence.

Unfortunately, we do not often allow the process to work because we confuse the visible signs of the healing process with the hurt itself, and try to stop it – 'Big boys don't cry' etc.

When the process is allowed to work consistently, people can re-emerge from all kinds of compulsions, addictions and confusions to a place where they are more able to use their intelligence and talents, where they can make better relationships with people, overcome their fears and most importantly, take control of their own lives. I have experienced this in my own life, and it has informed greatly the kind of parent I have been.

Many people instinctively know much of this to be true and consequently attempt to use attention as a healing tool, listening to friends in trouble, holding a crying child, making someone laugh, asking the right question to help someone think. These are all things we do for each other, because we like each other to do them for us. When any human interaction works, whether it be between a mother and her baby, a child and a teacher, a doctor and a patient, or two friends giggling into the night, it works because at least one person gives the other one attention, if only for a moment.

As the tools for inclusion develop, the awareness of the magical power of attention is growing. All of the methods which have been specifically designed to help people to think and plan for the restructuring of current institutions and services have, at their core, some form of structured attention. Through these everyone gets to be heard, and this is what makes the difference between *having* new information and being able to *put it into practice.*

From Transmitter to Receiver

In our unequal society, people get unequal access to attention. Without attention people do not do very well. Unloved babies do not thrive, and sometimes they die, despite being cared for in every other way. To de-value a person is to hurt them, and without attention it is hard to recover, or 'overcome' the hurt. De-valued people therefore often accumulate distress and their behaviour becomes more rigid, compulsive and 'attention seeking'. This makes them even more de-valued. They are then more likely to be labelled and medicated or punished than paid attention, thus adding to their hurt.

A group of people who are especially vulnerable to this lack of attention are people who cannot speak. Although there is no reason why one should have to be able to speak in order to communicate with each other - think of any baby you know - it seems that few people have the clarity of mind to observe and respond to the numerous non-verbal messages which such people are invariably throwing out.

Listening is more than pointing your ears in someone's direction and computing the words which come out of their mouths. Listening can mean going for a walk with someone and noticing what captures their interest. It can mean learning to recognise the situations in which a person becomes upset, or becomes animated; it can mean watching a persons movements, or the activities they choose over others; it can mean creating opportunities for that person to experience new things and observing their response. It can mean holding a person whilst they cry.

Giving attention (and using attention) are skills which can be learnt. Because we have not recognised the power of attention we have barely allowed our capacity to develop. It has been replaced by much less useful skills such as *telling* people what to think or do, giving them advice, or just doing things to each other with no explanation at all. This has shaped the "Outside-In" approach to service provision, and many people get paid a lot of money to do it, despite its ineffectiveness.

For inclusion to become a reality, many people who are trained to 'transmit' information have to transform their practice to become 'receivers'. They also have to learn to facilitate processes which intentionally give space and time to the thoughts and feelings of the oppressed.

The Small but Perfectly - Formed Question

Developing the skill of listening is enhanced by developing the skill of asking the right question.

From early childhood I loved to draw. Sometimes I drew all day. One of my best presents was a ream of white paper. Many people took a great deal of interest in my drawings and felt free to make all sorts of comments. The sort of thing they said was "How do you have the patience?", "How long did it take you?", "That bit is good," and the most common: "Me, I can't even draw a straight line, ha ha ha!" One day when I was about 20 years old, I took a newly framed copy of a drawing I had into a pub. A stranger in the pub asked if he could look at it, and after a while he asked, "Were you feeling a bit lost when you drew this?" I was startled, and looked again at my own picture. It was of Thumbelina (I am a very small person) alone on her waterlily. She is drifting down a stream with the help of a butterfly. The butterfly is attached to a ribbon which Thumbelina holds.

I had never before connected myself with this character in my drawing, but suddenly I could see exactly that I had drawn a picture of my life at that time. I realised that *no one had ever before asked me what my pictures meant to me.* I realised that all my pictures were me, trying to describe myself, but until that moment I had never had an aware audience, so I had never been able to make the connection. What that stranger had, was "attention". His attention allowed me to make a huge jump in my own understanding by asking me the right question.

At that moment the "Butterfly" came out of the Gents' toilet and we left, but I left a changed person.

Micheline

I have a much earlier memory of when I was in hospital. I was only a few days old, and the hospital had imparted to my parents the "news" that I was "congenitally handicapped" and probably wouldn't live. They told my parents to leave me in the hospital, to arrange for my christening, and to prepare themselves to lose me. My parents were obviously shocked and did not know how to argue with such professionalism, so they did what they were told. However, before he went, my father peered over the edge of my cot, and he looked at me with his sparkling green eyes, and he smiled at me.

His look said to me, "I know who you are, and I will come back for you." Because of that look, I decided not to give up and die. A few months later, he did indeed come back and take me home. He had "attention" for me, and it saved my life.

I remember these moments because they were comparatively rare, although many people fussed round me during my childhood. In fact, I recall being particularly annoyed when I asked an adult why my sister seemed so jealous of me, and they replied, "It's because you are disabled and get all the attention." If being shouted at and patted on the head by complete strangers in the street is something to be jealous of, I thought, then you do not understand anything!.

A good question is the best tool of empowerment because it reveals the person to themselves. All of the tools for Inclusion are based on carefully designed questions and the time and space for people to answer them, with the attention of others. The good question is the basis of all effective counselling, and also of the best teaching.

Questions have to be finely honed to work. One word can make a huge difference. "What do you think you will get out of this course" is not the same question as "What do you hope to get out of this course?"

Questions do not have to be asked in words. I discovered what my growing baby liked to eat for example, by offering her lots of different things to try and noting which ones she swallowed, and which ones she spat out.

My friend did not wait until her language-impaired daughter could say "Please stop sending me to that Special Unit" but recognised that she was answering the question "Do you like it at the Unit?" by coming off the bus everyday screaming.

The art of asking questions is rarely directly taught, but it should be. Most differences of opinion between people can be resolved by each asking the other questions, and listening to the answer, rather than by each arguing their point.

The Concept of Giftedness

Each person has a variety of ordinary and extraordinary gifts. The people who we call disabled are people who are missing some typical ordinary gifts. However, such people also have a variety of other ordinary and extraordinary gifts capable of stimulating interaction and meaning with others.

In fact it is not just that walking is a gift and not walking is not a gift., or that knowing how to put your clothes on right is a gift and not knowing how is not a gift. Rather walking is a gift and not walking is also a gift; knowing how to dress is a gift and not knowing how to dress is also a gift. Each creates the possibility of meaningful interaction.

Judith Snow [11]

Judith Snow is a travelling philosopher. In her book "What's Really Worth Doing and How to Do it", she has attempted to describe her concept of Giftedness. She tells the story of a young student she knew, who had a talent for diving. This talent was noticed and valued because it was thought that, if nurtured, it could lead to an Olympic Medal for Canada, where she lived.

Because of this hope, special resources were made available for her: swimming pools, diving boards, coaches; transport; flexible school time table; and so on. Her talent was treated as Gift to her Community. Judith, who has an impairment called Spinal Muscular Atrophy, who also could have done with some extra resources in order to live her life well, did not have them made available to her. The result was that for many years she was forced to live a life hidden away in hospital. Judith's impairment was certainly not seen as a Gift to the Community, only a burden. But Judith had friends and those friends helped her to see things differently.

Judith knew she had many thoughts and insights which were a direct result of her involuntary positioning on the margins of society and she began to see that her perspective could have a value to her community if only she could be more connected. In fact, she began to compare what she called the students' 'ability to park herself upside down in water' to what she felt she had to offer, and became quite angry. One day she hired some transport, took herself from her hospital ward to her friends' house, demanded to be put to bed there, and refused to speak for more than two weeks. Her friends were thus forced to stop muttering powerlessly about the injustices of Judith'situation, but to share the responsibility for setting her free. They formed what they called the 'Joshua Committee' and together found the resources that were needed for Judith to leave the hospital and to start to live a life.

She is now a well known international speaker, writer and facilitator within the inclusion movement. The change occurred when her unique experience of life was seen as a gift.

The response of her friends to what they felt to be an unjust situation led not only to the creation of the Joshua Committee, but consequently to the development of 'Circles of Support', which have themselves affected positively every member of every circle, It goes on outwards, like ripples in a lake. And Judith gained a voice in the world.

The concept of Giftedness is not as simple as 'look at the abilities, not the disabilities', although that is in itself a good thing. It is looking at the disabilities as an opportunity to create a new response which will lead to learning and growth for the whole community. If we take this attitude towards our unsolved problems, then the life of anyone who presents such 'problems' has a value - a meaning.

The Transference of Resources

If the Government has enough money to explode nuclear bombs, why doesn't it have money to build schools?

Boy speaking to the Education Secretary, New Delhi 1999

"Not enough money" is never the real issue when we are talking about inclusion. The real issue is always priorities.

There are still an estimated 275 million children in the world who receive less than four years formal education because of poverty. The World Conference on Education for All in Thailand, 1990, set a target date for universal primary education by the year 2000. The best estimate of the price of this is $8 billion dollars a year – half of what Americans spend on toys each year, four days of global military spending, or nine minutes of international currency speculation. Bill Gates could fund it out of his own pocket. (Source: the New Internationalist August 1999). We are a long way from achieving this goal.

In the developed world, millions and millions of pounds are spent on medical model provision. The medical model is very expensive to run. It takes armies of assessors, managers, therapists, monitors, gatekeepers, administrators, experts, drivers, care-staff, fund-raisers, research scientists, charity workers and service-providers of all kinds, yet most disabled people remain poor, unemployed and constantly waiting for help.

Disabled people have agreed that we need to get the resources which are swallowed up by this giant system *redirected* into our own hands so that we can buy the help we need directly. We believe that together we can create the support structures for all disabled people to manage such resources themselves, with appropriate help. To this end we fought for and achieved the 'Direct Payments Bill' 1996 which allows local authorities to put the money for the support we need into our own bank account, or that of a local organisation of disabled people, from which we can pay personal assistants to work for us, helping us manage our daily lives as we choose to live them.

The biggest excuse for not including disabled people in ordinary life is the 'cost implications', but we are not asking for additional resources.

We do not want the medical model to continue. We want the resources transferred from funding perpetual failure, to funding inclusive communities. In a global sense, we want the priorities to change from funding greed, to funding equality.

The Re-building of Community

While we have reached the limits of institutional problem-solving, we are only at the beginning of exploring a new vision for community. It is a vision of regeneration. It is a vision of re-associating the exiled. It is a vision of freeing ourselves from service and advocacy. It is a vision of centring our lives in community

John McKnight – The Careless Society [12]

Many places in the world, have now rejected full-frontal Free-Marketeering, (although not capitalism itself). Once people feet the full brunt of de-regulation, there seems to be a common revulsion resulting in the dismissing of the Governments which have been elected to carry it out. The real human need for security cannot be answered by such economic policies. The problem is that many of the reforms put in place in the free-marketeering years are very difficult to reverse, which ever government is in power. The hope lies in our ability to recreate communities within which the most vulnerable of us can be protected whilst we work out how to manage our international economies in sustainable ways. The far-seeing service providers who saw their clients living in 'institutions without walls' began to see if it were possible to enable their clients to become the catalysts for the intentional re-building of community.

Community Guides

Most guides are people with a special eye for the gift, the potential, the interest, the skills, the smile, the capacity of those said to be 'in special need'. Focussing upon these strengths, they introduce people into community life. They report that their most basic change in attitude which allowed them to be a guide, was to stop trying to 'fix' people.

John Mcknight [13]

They began by assuming that the need for love, friendship, home and meaningful occupation are universal human needs, irrespective of age, class, race or disability. They then looked to find 'spaces' within the local community in which their clients would be welcome, and in which they could pursue their interests and develop their skills. They worked to help ordinary people recognise that they had just what their client needed, and often accompanied their client into that space to facilitate the interaction. In many instances finding a place where someone could do something which they really liked doing, turned into a voluntary, or even a paid job. Once in the job, relationships with co-workers would develop and other things would happen 'naturally'. Helping people to choose where to live and who to live with, even if it meant a full-time live-in assistant living with them, was the focus of much of their early work, helping to develop relationships with their neighbours, and 'mainstream' facilities such as cafes or clubs.

They helped facilitate ongoing support for their clients by bringing together the people who cared about them into 'circles of support' - voluntary associations of people including family members, paid assistants, friends and neighbours who agreed to focus their attention on this one person who would rely on their co-operation to live a meaningful life. Within such circles everyone got a chance to reveal themselves, their dreams and their vulnerabilities, and got the chance to work as a team to make at least one persons life better. Usually of course, everyone gained support and friendship from belonging to the circle, and went on to form their own circles. Some people call this 'villaging'

Guides do not make themselves indispensable to their 'clients'. Their goal is to enable interdependent relationships between excluded people and their local communities. Guides learnt that they must leave the scene before the excluded become wholly incorporated as citizens.

(It is important to note that this movement distinguishes between 'disabling' services and those which clearly support community life such as Personal Assistants, equipment and adaptations which aid independent living, and specialised medical services)

Notes Section Two

1 Mike Green, quoted in *What's Really Worth Doing And How To Do It*, Judith Snow, Inclusion Press 1998

2 Quote from Pippa Murray and Jill Penman (Eds), *Let Our Children Be*, Parents With Attitude (Pubs) 1996

3 *Changing Our School*, Highfield Junior School 1997

4 Jane Campbell and Mike Oliver, *Disability Politics*, Routledge 1996

5 *A Sense of Self*, Camerawork 1988

6 ibid

7 *Flying Pigs* 1999, The Alliance for Inclusive Education

8 Sue Napolitano *A Dangerous Woman* 1995, The Greater Manchester Coalition of Disabled People.

9 *Flying Pigs* 1998, The Alliance for Inclusive Education

10 O' Brien, O' Brien and Jacobs, *Celebrating the Ordinary*, Inclusion Press 1998

11 Judith Snow, *What's Really Worth Doing and How to Do It*, Inclusion Press

12 John McKnight *The Careless Society- Community and its Counterfeits* Basic Books 1995

13 ibid

INCLUSIVE EDUCATION

Our goal should be clear. We are seeking nothing less than a life surrounded by the richness and diversity of community. A collective life. A common life. An everyday life. A powerful life that gains its joy from the creativity and connectedness that come when we join in association to create an inclusive world

John McKnight [1]

The fact that 'guides' had to work so hard to create welcoming spaces for adults, and that those adults were unnecessarily damaged by years of exclusion and low-expectations, and that 'ordinary' people were inordinately frightened and lacking in self-confidence in their ability to relate to disabled people, naturally led them to question whether it would not be better to start with children and children's services before such harm had been inflicted. Many people, including disabled people, parents, educationalists and service providers realised that the habits of exclusion are learned when we are children, and are very difficult to unlearn when we become adults. Therefore it was imperative that schools became the foundation for building inclusive communities. The term 'Inclusive Education' was born.

Special Education is Based on the Medical Model of Disability and Behaviour

There is nothing special about special schools except that they offer fewer opportunities.

**A physiotherapist in a special school,
during a conversation with the author.**

In Britain certainly, the medial model is still the dominant model within the education system. The legal definition of 'Special Educational Needs 'puts the problem firmly within the child, stating that a child has a learning difficulty if they need support which is 'Not normally provided for children of the same age' (1996 Education Act). Instead of expanding what is 'normally provided' to cater for a greater diversity of need, an individualised package of support is drawn up for the child. This leads to the current process of assessments, diagnosis, individual education programmes, specialist help, and possible removal from mainstream into a separate school or unit, all focused on 'treating' the child's defects, not the defects of the system. The concept of the 'Continuum of Provision' is the medical model institutionalised - the child is moved to the (fixed) provision as deemed necessary by the experts. The law in Britain (1999) still upholds the power of local authorities to compel children into separate provision if they believe it to be 'appropriate' and 'cost-effective'. This is why it is a segregated system in the true sense of the word.

Segregated schools may be beautiful safe buildings, with high ratio of committed staff and all the state-of-the-art technology, but they cannot equip young disabled people to live a valued life in the community. They fail their pupils academically (only 4% gained 5 GCSEs in 1997) and perhaps even more importantly, they cannot build relationships with non-disabled friends because there are no non-disabled children in their schools. Likewise they cannot teach 'life-skills' because life involves other people. Furthermore, it instils in young children who are not disabled the idea that their disabled brothers sisters and friends, *do not need them*. This is probably the single most harmful idea of all. It is also the *most untrue*.

Inclusion Must be Intentional

Inclusion makes us think deeply about what we want our world to be. Who do we want as neighbours. What do we want our communities, churches, synagogues, mosques and schools to look like?

Marsha Forest and Jack Pearpoint

It will not do to throw people who have been traditionally segregated from mainstream society into mainstream schools or communities with a few extra resources and to think this is inclusion. The habits and structures built up over a hundred years of segregation will still dominate the experience unless there is a deliberate drawing of attention to doing things differently. In order to carry this out successfully it is necessary to state the reasons why, to create and agree upon new and explicit common goals.

Schools have to decide on their purpose, and look at their management and organisation to see if they meet their purpose, and how you enable that to take place. For example, inclusion has to happen in everything we say or do. It can't just be added on, and that is why it shouldn't be called integration. Inclusion is more powerful, because it means you take the needs of all children, particularly those who are most vulnerable because of their gender or their circumstances or their learning needs or whatever, and you say 'How does the institution enable that child to come to school and be happy and feel "Oh its great, I'll have some good fun at school today and I'm going to learn at the same time with my friends.

Brigid - Headteacher, Cleves School [2]

Disability Equality Training helps people to see the connection between the medical model of disability and 'Special Education'. It also helps people to begin to perceive of an education system based on the social model of disability.

Integration is not Inclusion

It is quite possible to transfer the philosophy and practice of 'special education' and the medical model into mainstream schools and think you have done inclusion:

The action plan was formed at our last meeting. It came about when Maresa, a disabled and very important member of our group, stressed she was very unhappy at her school, because, although her school was mainstream, she was still being badly excluded and she asked for our help.

Maresa had a hopeless head of Special Educational Needs at her school who had some very strange and annoying ideas about what would benefit Maresa and the other students. For example, Maresa spent the first week of term alone in a specially built room in case she frightened the other children. Her SENCO said

"They have to get used to her being in the building before they actually see her, they might get scared!" Her SENCO does not believe that Maresa can communicate either, although Maresa has proved that she can use a letterboard. This proves how little the SENCO understands about the capabilities of young disabled people.

Another bad thing was that when Maresa gave out invitations to an Easter party to friends at school, the school stopped her, saying it was too soon for the children to be involved with Maresa and that it was up to them to decide when steps like that were to be taken forward.

Maresa only spends five lessons a week in a normal classroom with her peers out of forty lessons, although her Statement says that the best way for her to learn is to be with, and able to observe, other young people.

Young and Powerful, planning and action 1997

Integration is a necessary precursor to inclusion because, obviously, the children have to be physically present before anything can happen. However, the creation of an inclusive school requires the systematic dismantling of the medical model of disability (and behaviour) and the restructuring of the whole school to embrace the social model.

Principles of Cleves School:

All children have the right to access to the whole school curriculum;

Children and adults learn best in an environment where they feel valued, accepted and respected;

Discrimination undermines both perpetrators' and victims' ability to achieve: our curriculum, relationships and organisation must challenge this and present positive images and practices;

All adults and children who enter our school have equal worth.

Learning and Inclusion, The Cleves School Experience

This is a process which takes time, and which must involve staff, parents and pupils in creating a common dream (The Mission Statement). Creating this mission statement is the first step to creating community.

All Means All

When viewed from the medical model, it is very difficult to imagine the most 'severely' affected children, whether their problem is deemed to be physical, intellectual or emotional, having their needs met within mainstream schools or communities. Consequently many people who understand the concept of integration, still believe there are limits to the kind of child for whom it is suitable. It is actually quite amusing how varied these imagined limits are from person to person, school to school, or authority to authority. Nottingham LEA for example began its 'Inclusion Programme' with children with Moderate learning difficulties and Behaviour Difficulties (because these were the numerically biggest groups) whilst physically disabled children and children with the label of Severe Learning Difficulties were deemed too difficult, whilst at the same time Tower Hamlets LEA was busy emptying its schools for physically disabled children as long as they *didn't* have learning difficulties. The reason people have this Imagination Difficulty is that the medical model, in which we are all steeped, has the wrong goals.

Inclusive education has as its goal the development of relationships which are mutually supportive, and which draw people into a collective life. It recognises therefore that the people who have the greatest need for support, have the greatest need for 'inclusion'. It also recognises that it is the presence of people whose needs *cannot* be met by existing mainstream practices which creates the catalyst for the change from 'integration' to 'inclusion' - CHANGE being the operative word:

Before Eddie was diagnosed as autistic, he followed on from his older brother into our local playgroup. It was then that I realised that the other children were helping him to learn. They taught him the routines of playgroup, appropriate behaviours (and sometimes inappropriate behaviours) and how to socialise with other children. They used skills only children can use - gestures, looks, manoeuvring him physically. Because Ed's progress at the playgroup was so dramatic, this made me determine that he would attend a mainstream school. Up until then I could only think of the obstacles against him attending mainstream, his lack of speech and unusual and at times extreme behaviours...Before Eddie's starting day at the school there was good communication between me and the school. To make his first days run smoothly we talked about Eddy's likes and dislikes, what upset him and what helped him to calm down, how to help him settle with as little stress as possible. At that time Ed refused to dress and undress himself so we made sure his first day wasn't a PE day. He hated the feel and smell of playdough, so the teacher provided alternatives for Eddie and the other children.

Although his needs were being looked at and addressed, I wanted Eddie to be treated the same as everybody else and this means he had to conform to the group as much as he can, for example sitting on chairs on the carpet with the rest of the class. Other times this is achieved with the school changing their methods. In reception Eddie needed a photo of himself above his peg so that he would know where it was as he could not recognise his name at the time. So Mrs Alexandra (the Headteaher) gave permission for everybody else in the school to have a photograph of themselves above their peg which all of the children enjoyed. Ed was not being singled out as different or separate, and I have found out that it is things like this which stop the children treating him too differently.

Suzanne Webb, speech at the Altogether Now Conference, Redbridge Parents in Partnership 1998

Many of the parents who have fought the hardest for their child to be included in their local mainstream school have children with these 'severe' labels, and it has been this which has baffled the authorities most. They have not understood that the parents have rejected the false goal of the medical model, and are pursuing a different agenda, a different future outcome. This is why inclusion has to be a conscious process in which such issues are examined and some common understandings reached. Without this it will be impossible for practitioners to know whether or not they are being successful (a common difficulty within 'integrated' schools).

Friendship, An Over-riding Need of All Young People

A recent series of programmes on BBC2 on bullying, told the stories of children who had committed suicide. The viewers were led to believe that there were in fact four suicides, but in the last few minutes a girl appeared, having been saved by emergency treatment, to tell her own tale. She said that when she had been given the lead part in the school play "Annie", her friends, in their jealousy, had turned against her. *"Without my friends I am nothing."* she said to explain her massive overdose of paracetamol.

Recent research carried out by the Bolton 'Data for Inclusion Project' asked children in 500 primary and secondary schools what made them happy or unhappy at school, and what makes a good or bad teacher:

An overwhelming majority, (62.8%) of the 2,527 children surveyed said that it was 'friends' that made them happy at school. There was specific mention of particular friendships but also friendly teachers and other friendly pupils. Feeling safe, making other children happy and being trusted by others also added to their happiness

Joe Whittaker, John Kenworthy and Colin Crabtree [3]

Yet school, which is the place we send our children to be prepared for adult life, treats friendship as a rather unimportant by-product of the fact that all young people have to be there to get their "education". In fact, friendship amongst young people is almost seen as threatening by adults, who are usually greatly outnumbered in classrooms and schools, and feel they have to keep control. We all know it's easier to control single individuals than large groups, especially if those large groups have commitment and loyalty to each other, and see adults as an oppressive force in their lives.

Friendship in Jeopardy

Children who are officially excluded from school, not by other children, but by the education system itself, are even more deeply affected by general lack of support for their friendships than most. This includes disabled children and children with learning difficulties or emotional and behavioural problems.

The medical model of disability, in its fixation on the impairment, has simply ignored the issue of friendship in its definition of "Special Educational Needs". In fact, because of its eugenic roots, much of the thinking behind the Special Education System assumes peer relationships between disabled and non-disabled young people to be undesirable, or impossible. They believe that the disabled children will compare themselves unfavourably to the more able children, and will suffer loss of self-esteem and self-confidence if they are not kept apart. Generally, they simply cannot imagine a non-disabled child gaining anything from a relationship with a disabled child, except perhaps useful experience leading towards a job in the caring professions. They are genuinely confounded by what they see happening in inclusive schools. For example, Kenn Jupp describes the reaction of pupils in mainstream primary schools towards a child who had transferred from his school for children with severe learning difficulties:

Everyone wanted to be with her at once, it seemed, wherever she was. Order was maintained by a class teacher who very soon had to insist on a rota system for those who wanted to sit next to her at lunch time. We were a little perturbed by this, as we did not want Lauren to become the classroom pet, along with the hamster and goldfish. Whilst we much preferred the other children to show their interest and give their support rather than avoiding and isolating Lauren, by the same token we did not want her to become a novelty or curiosity which wore off after a week or so. As it happened we need not have concerned ourselves; three years on the situation is much the same and a strong bond has been formed between Lauren and her classmates. As for the rota system, it still has to be implemented since her popularity has not waned...

Recently the teacher had a deputation of Lauren's classmates who had learned that she was about to be admitted to hospital for a while in order to undergo a surgical operation on her legs.

"Is this to make Lauren's feet look like our feet?" they asked, "Or is it so that she will be able to walk better?" Before the teacher could reply, they went on "Because if it is to make her feet look like ours, we are quite happy with them the way they are, thankyou!

Kenn Jupp [4]

Special education tends to replace peer relationships with adult professionals and other paid workers. The child is often placed with other children with similar types and levels of impairments to their own. In this situation it can be almost impossible for the children ever to do things together without adult supervision and intervention, because the children simply cannot facilitate each other. It is difficult for them to become part of a young people's culture, and to learn the "language" of youth. This makes "integration" later on at home, college or work, very hard. Most young people who have grown up in segregated schools or homes, find that they are always more comfortable in the company of other separated people. This is as true for non-disabled children without parents, brought up in children's homes and residential schools as it is for disabled children brought up in special schools. Re-entry into mainstream life is possible, but extremely difficult.

Friendship as an Educational Goal

There remain many skills Shawntell has yet to master, such as independent toileting and eating, verbal communication, and walking with stability. However, despite our active efforts to help her in these areas, whether Shawntell achieves these skills in her lifetime is not what concerns us most as parents. Our biggest concern is that there will be no-one in Shawntells life who wants to be with her, that she will be at risk of being victimised, that she will be lonely and that she will be without friends.

Jeff Tully – speech at a conference on inclusion , Essex, 1998

Jeff Tully believes the friendship should be an educational goal, equal to literacy and numeracy. As friendship is young people's greatest need, and therefore greatest interest, this should be much easier than trying to install enthusiasm about quadratic equations. It is about harnessing all the energy that goes into running up their parents' phone bills, into building a truly supportive learning community.

Friendship Needs Support

The culture in schools will reflect that of the wider community if left to itself. The market-place ideology that dominates most cultures, except those which are still deeply religious, is based on competition. It is not at all surprising therefore that even very young children start to rank themselves and others according to how valued are the adults-they-will-be. Research has shown for example, that by the age of three, children of all races value their white friends more highly than they value their black friends. It is still common in playgrounds in British schools to hear girls of eight of nine being called slags, sluts, or bitches, and for children to sing rhymes about poorer children who buy their clothes in Tesco.

In her book "You Can't Say You Can't Say Play", Vivien Paley describes her attempt to combat this ranking in her nursery class. She asked herself the question of whether they should have a rule which says "You can't say 'You can't play'". She wondered if it would stop the dominance of the majority by the few children already seen as the "bosses", or whether it was an unenforceable rule. She went and asked lots of older children what they thought, and they said "It's too late for us, we don't trust adults anymore, but the little ones still give you the benefit of the doubt. Yes, you should introduce the rule." So she did. The rule was written up and stood on the piano, but if people broke the rule they didn't get punished. The real point was to become conscious of their own behaviours towards each other, and to ask themselves if it was "fair". Children do like fairness, and so when their teacher noticed someone excluding a child, even in quite subtle ways, she brought them altogether to talk about it, in relation to the rule. Within a very short time, the children were "policing" the rule themselves. Vivien Paley described the children feeling "relieved", especially the "bosses". It was as though the rule had rescued them from a force which came from outside of themselves, but which they did not know how to resist.

Parents As Allies

As well as the many things which schools can do to move in this direction, young people need the support of their parents to help achieve this goal.

Currently, the way we live supports isolation, not friendship. 'Playing out' is almost impossible for most children because the environment has become too dangerous. Mum is no longer in the kitchen making tea but out at work.. Young people are dependent on adults until they are surprisingly old! They often cannot travel around independently and are reliant on being given lifts. They often cannot ask who they want home but are restricted by who their parents will allow them to invite. They often cannot choose where to go because they cannot pay for it, or it meets with their parents' disapproval. Very often, their time is managed by their parents, so that any independent arrangements they make with their friends may have to be cancelled or altered at the last moment. Even worse, adults may decide to move house without any real recognition that they are, in effect, breaking up relationships which are of the utmost importance to the young people involved. In fact, children's relationships outside the family are generally treated as if they are of little importance, as if they are not real, or easily replaceable. This is not so.

It is because of this unaware attitude towards peer relationships when we are young that we grow up to become such isolated and socially inept adults, guarded about giving or receiving support from each other. We are pressurised then to see one-to-one sexual relationships as the only route to fulfilling our emotional need for security. The one-in-three breakdown rate of such relationships shows how this hope is so unrealistic.

Every child is my child.

The fragmentation of tribes and communities into nuclear families, now often with only one adult taking the full responsibility for bringing up a family is a highly 'unnatural' state when compared to our thousands of year's history.

This 'model' makes life for parents and children very difficult, even when everyone is fit, well, emotionally stable, in school or in work, and well-housed. However, as soon as life's messy troubles hit us, as is inevitable, such a model is totally inadequate. The ultimate victims are our children. All of the children who are currently excluded from schools, or are in danger of exclusion, come from situations in which the 'family' structure has been unable to cope with the challenges life has thrown their way. Either the adult relationships have broken down, or material resources have run out, or illness, or impairments or death have placed intolerable hardship on the 'unit', so the 'unit' can no longer cope.

What this means is that we all meet children whose needs are not being met. We meet them in school, in local authority homes, on the street, in our own houses when our children invite them in. or we see them on buses, being driven away to 'special' places where 'special' people are paid to look after them.

It is interesting to note that many parents of disabled children, who want to support their child's inclusion into their local community, have had to make the decision to 'open up' their home to local children. More importantly, we have to hang around as an adult 'resource' – to lift and carry, facilitate communication, and to supply the crisps and drinks. Many of us have been shocked to realise how rare it is for young people to be offered even this little amount of attention. We have inadvertently found our homes becoming 'safe-houses' and refuges for children escaping neglect and abuse at home. The problem is that we are ourselves so under-resourced, that there is not much we can do to help, even when we have wanted to. I think we could all confess to at times feeling overwhelmed and chucking all the kids back out onto the street again.

It has struck me, however, that a small amount of support would make a lot of difference to my ability to act responsibly towards some of these children. For example, money for extra food would have meant that I could have fed the child who came night after night at around dinner time, or fifteen minutes babysitting from a neighbour could have enabled me to accompany the ten year old home in the dark. Shared out, the responsibility for each other's children, would be possible. The first step would be to adopt in our hearts the attitude that 'every child is my child'. Then we could start to think creatively about how we can put our collective resources to bear, not simply on the 'call in Social Services!' crisis type management of a problem-gone-too-far, but on supporting natural relationships within a community to a much greater extent.

The inadequacy of our response to young people and their need to have and to be friends, is brought into painful consciousness by loving a child who is lonely. The choice now being made by many parents and children to reject the segregated system and to bring their disabled children out into their local community, has shown that everyone has to be involved in an explicit and conscious change of priorities if it is to work.

My own daughter has had many invitations home from her school friends, only to find that the friends' parents have said no. They had said their house is not accessible for her wheelchair, or that she might get hurt by their dog, or they are afraid of lifting her wrong, or they don't have time to go and pick her up in their car.

The most common reason is that they are too busy to help and wouldn't it be better if their child(ren) came to my house instead? Which is usually what happens. However, this can only happen because I have made supporting my daughter's friendships a priority.

My decision to be available to them with my van and lots of pasta and pizzas for at least some of the time has made me realise how abandoned many young feel especially once they become teenagers. Because I get to hang around with them I hear about their lives.

This problem would be lessened by involving all parents in the debate about inclusion. If a school were to put forward a mission statement which included "Friendship as an Education Goal", and parents of children with 'special needs were encouraged to ask for the support they need from other parents, a new collective response could be designed in which all children would benefit.

Effective Education

In the 21st Century, world class standards will demand that everyone is:

Highly literate

Highly numerate

Well informed

Capable of learning constantly

Confident and able to play their part as citizens of a democratic society

In addition, a world class education service would have to provide all pupils, whatever their backgrounds, with the opportunity to become:

Highly expert in one or more fields

Highly creative and innovative

Capable of leadership

**Michael Barber, Head of Standards and Effectiveness Unit, DFEE 1998
(North of England Education Conference 1998)**

The Self – We value ourselves as unique human beings capable of spiritual moral, intellectual and physical growth and development.

Relationships – We value others for themselves, not only for what they have or what they can do for us.

Society –We value truth, freedom, justice, human rights, the rule of law and collective effort for the common good.

In particular we value families as sources of love and support for all their members, and as a basis of a society in which people care for others.

The Environment – We value the environment, both natural and shaped by humanity, as the basis of life and a source of wonder and inspiration.

**The Qualifications and Curriculum Authority-
Preparing Young People for Adult Life. May 1999**

These two apparently conflicting statements illustrate the worry many people feel that the perceived need to 'drive up standards' is at odds with the development of inclusive education. However, the evidence is that standards in such skills as literacy and numeracy do improve within inclusive school systems such as that developed in the London Borough of Newham. Newham is an inner-city Education Authority which has pioneered inclusive education in Britain. Following a ten year plan, Newham has closed all but one of their segregated schools and transferred the resources into mainstream, inclusive provision. Far from compromising 'standards', 1n 1998 Newham was applauded by the National League Tables as the 'Most Improved' LEA in Britain. It is also evident that it does not entail the unacceptable price of rising exclusions, enforced segregation, or escalating costs.

What is of concern to many is the obsession of most Governments of the developed world with the promotion of tools which, although genuinely aimed at an 'equal opportunities agenda' have been developed by practitioners of our past, faulty eugenics - based education system: Standardised Testing, Setting, Selective (specialist) schools, etc. Alan Stoskopf, in his paper 'The Forgotten History of Eugenics' speaks for many of us when he says:

Even if many supporters of high-stakes tests might recoil at the assumptions underlying the use of standardised tests earlier in this century, the consequences of this kind of educational reform might not be so different from the 1920s. This becomes even more apparent when performances are compared between poorer and more affluent school districts. Doing well on these tests is strongly correlated with income levels and only reconfirms the educational inequities that have characterised (American) education throughout the century. The academic tracking begun by yesterday's eugenicists is an institutional legacy we live with today. Education reform that is driven by high-stakes tests stands a good chance of entrenching that legacy.

Alan Stoskopf-'Rethinking Schools' Vol.13 1999

Tools for Inclusion

There is a Celtic rune of hospitality which declares 'I put food in the eating place, water in the drinking place and music in the listening place....in order to welcome the stranger'

I suggest in order to rebuild this sorry society of ours we have to put disabled people, the Native American (or Australian), the elder, the excluded in the listening place. We have to slow down and listen at a new and deep level. (Some adults have begun to listen to their young ones this way and learned it is the little one, not the grown up who is the authority).

To listen like this, lengthily and slowly is diametrically opposite to oppressive behaviour. I think we have humbly to be prepared to be told to do things differently, because we do not know some things. We need to be willing to be taught a different language and pace so that we may become the richer.

We are going to learn to receive help where we never once thought it necessary.

Josephine Saunders – Thoughts on Inclusion 1998.

In contrast to the tools developed by the educators and doctors of the early part of this century, new tools are being developed by people who are finding ways to make inclusion a reality in modern schools and communities. This recognises that we are in a process of transition from one 'world view' to another. Each of these tools has incorporated a form of 'structured listening' as a key to change.

Circle Time

Circle time is where everybody in a class sits down in a circle, including the teacher or facilitator, and takes turns to speak whilst everybody listens:

Corinne: "Some people easily make lots of friends, but other feel lonely and worry that no-one likes them. It can then be much harder for them to learn and work well. They are likely to mess about and annoy or hurt other people. Circle time can help everyone know and like everyone in the class more, and want to help each other.

Headteacher: Everyone learns that what they have to say is valid, valuable and valued by the others in the class or group – even if their wish is simply to say "pass". Children were learning that they had a right to a say – but not the right to be right".

Corinne: we made our class rules so we don't hurt each other….

Greg: Then we talk about our arguments and problems and we sort them out. We talk about bad things that happened, calling names, fighting, someone annoying us, scabbing food and trying to get our lunch. If a name is brought up and they say 'it's not me. It's someone else', we ask them for the truth. We ask if someone else saw what happened, and we talk about what needs to be done. If bullying still happens, we call in mediation to sort it out"

Pupils and Teachers, Highfield Junior School [5]

Mediation

Mediation is a technique and set of skills which can be taught to children to help them resolve difficulties between them without adult intervention:

Carla and Adam had a row. Ryan and Maya were mediators. They all sat down with Ryan and Maya in the middle.

First Ryan went through the rules, and checked that Carla and Adam agreed to keep them and wanted to solve the conflict. Ryan thanked them for coming to talk.

Maya turned to Carla and said "What happened?"

When Carla had told her side, Maya said it back to her to check that she had got it right,

Then Ryan asked Adam "What happened?" and when Adam had finished Ryan checked back what he had said.

Then Maya asked them both in turn "How do you feel?" and "How do you think the other person feels?" and they talked about their feelings.

Next Ryan asked "Why did you fall out do you think?". After they had talked about that Maya asked "And what are you going to do about it?"

Ryan asked Carla to say all the ways they could think of for solving the row, how they could be friends and how they could avoid having the same row again.

Then Ryan said "Thank you for all your ideas. This is what you have said you will do. Do you both agree?

"Yes" said Carla.

"Well" said Adam, "I suppose we could try it".

"Good, and thank you for talking honestly" said Ryan and Maya.

"Let's meet next week to see how it worked".

The next week had been better, but there were still some problems. Ryan and Maya asked them in turn "How did you get on" and "What might work better instead?"

Pupils at Highfield Junior School [6]

Guardian Angels

Guardian Angels are a form of peer support:

Headteacher: "Guardian Angels came from the idea that you can fly to someone's rescue and guard them. It was a way of taking circle time out into the playground and having peer support. It meant that someone would be there to support you.

A child who is trying to change their behaviour may choose up to three guardian angels to fly into situations which they cannot handle. I'd say everyone in the school has been a guardian angel at some time. They report on any progress to the class, and the class rewards the guardian angels.

Alan: Guardian angels are there to help you. They might be your friend or someone else. You can have two or three guardian angels. If you are being bullied they fly to your rescue and mediate the problem. If you are trying to improve your behaviour, they are around to help you.

Pupils at Highfield Junior School [7]

Circles of Friends

'Circles of Friends' is a tool originally designed by John O'Brien, Jack Pierpoint, Marsha Forrest and Judith Snow in Canada, to help smooth the transition from separate to inclusive provision. Its purpose is to help children who are particularly vulnerable to being isolated or lonely, or who may not have had the chance to develop self-confidence or social skills because they have been placed in segregated settings in the past.

As facilitators they developed 'lessons' on building circles of friends. They helped children to draw diagrams of all the relationships they had in their lives, from the very closest to the most formal – the people who were paid to be in their lives. They were asked to talk about these different relationships, and then asked to imagine how they would feel if they had only a very few people in their 'inner' friendship circles, and many people in their outer 'professional' circles. Having decided that they would feel 'dreadful' if this was their life, they were asked to brainstorm ideas as to what they could do to support someone who had lived a very isolated life to 'fill up' their circles so that their lives were better. The young people were bursting with ideas and there were many volunteers to form circles around individual children. With the help of an adult facilitator these volunteers intentionally set out to make sure that the focus child was able to feel wanted and able to take part in whatever they chose. They made sure for example, that the child was telephoned at home at least once a week, and that they were invited out sometimes at weekends. They were not asked to be the 'best mates' of the child, but to help make the opportunities for that child to make their own friends. In John McKnights' words, they were learning to be 'Community Guides', helping to draw the child into associational life. This tool is now being used with great success in North America, Britiain and Australia.

MAPs

MAP stands for Making an Action Plan. It is a tool designed to help a child make a transition from segregated to inclusive schooling, or when first entering the education system, or when transferring from primary to secondary school, or school to college etc. It starts with an invited group of people who have a relationship with the child and who will be involved in the child's life as friends, family, teachers, therapists, personal assistants and so on. The MAP is facilitated by someone familiar with the procedure, and is recorded in words and pictures. It is a form of 'social model' assessment.

The big question that frames the MAP is asked of the child and their parents "What kind of future do you want? The MAP process means Making an Action Plan, but it is also like a map – you have a destination in mind, a starting point, and you work out a possible route, to stop yourself getting lost.

The MAP facilitator asks everyone the same questions:

- *The history told by the family*
- *What is your dream (the destination at age 25)*
- *What is your nightmare (so you can avoid it)*
- *Who are you (one-word descriptions)*
- *What are your strengths and gifts*
- *What are your needs*
- *How shall we plan to build on the strengths, avoid the pits, answer the needs*

**Mary A. Falvey, Marsha Forest, Jack Pearpoint
and Richard L. Rosenberg** [8]

The power of the MAP is that it breaks the isolation of the family and sets up a 'team' who have a common goal in mind. Without this piece of planning, the child and their parents will not feel that they have been 'heard', or that they can be active participants in the child's education. It also creates a framework for teachers and others to judge 'success', especially for children with more 'severe' or 'complex' impairments for whom having a circle of friends could possibly be the main goal of their placement, as opposed to GCSE maths, or being able to independently make a cheese sandwich.

Emotional Literacy

We should spend less time ranking children and more time helping them to identify their natural competencies and gifts, and cultivate those. There are hundred and hundreds of ways to succeed, and many, many more different abilities that will help you get there.

Howard Gardner - Project Spectrum

Studies are now showing clear evidence that a high IQ in childhood is not a reliable indicator of success in adult life. For example, George Valliant of Harvard University Medical school, carried out a longitudinal study following ninety-five Harvard students from the 1940's into middle age.[41] He found that the men with the highest test scores in college were not particularly successful compared to their lower-scoring peers in terms of salary, productivity or status in their field. Nor did they have the greatest life satisfaction, nor the most happiness with friendships, family and romantic relationships. Similarly, a study into middle age of 450 boys from a slum in Somerville, Massachusetts,[10] showed that levels of long term unemployment were the same across the IQ spectrum. In both cases it was shown the difference between success and failure was related to other childhood abilities, such as being able to handle frustrations, understand emotions and get on with people.

As illustrated by Michael Barbers' vision of a world class education system', many national governments fear that their citizens will be excluded from the 'Global Market' if they do not perform better than their competitors in certain 'core' skills. This is persuading parents and teachers to focus their child's attention, like an ever-shrinking spotlight on reading, writing and mathematics, and judging success solely in terms of examination grades. Without an equal emphasis on emotional intelligence, on self-esteem and the ability to make and be friends, the alternative vision illustrated by the Qualifications and Curriculum Association, will have no chance.

According to Daniel Goleman in his book 'Emotional Intelligence,'[11] this will require an "Expanded mission for schools". This mission requires a return to the classic role of education, in which schools are explicit agents of society, making sure that children learn essential life skills.

We all have the capacity for emotional intelligence, regardless of our other abilities or impairments. However, for this potential to develop we all need opportunities and support. Ideally, we would all be born to perfect parents, who themselves were parented perfectly. They would have endless time and patience to respond to our need for food, warmth, cuddles, play, information. We would receive hundred of positive messages a day as feedback to our little initiatives. Consequently, we would grow up secure, self-assured, self-aware, empathetic, zestful, loving and bursting with enthusiasm about life and our part in it. But as we all know, this rarely happens. All parents are battle-scarred and weary and in any case, child rearing is a community affair, too demanding for one or two adults to succeed at alone.

However, it is gradually being realised that emotional intelligence can be taught or reclaimed at any age and this is a far more successful strategy than blame, punishment or exclusion in helping people with emotional or behavioural difficulties. This realisation has led to the inclusion of Emotional Literacy Courses in nurseries and schools. There are many developing attempts to teach emotional literacy. They have common factors which have been shown to make a difference:

1. Helping children to recognise and name different feelings which they have ("I feel angry!")

2. Helping children recognise facial expressions and tones of voice which match these feelings

3. Helping children to 'read' these signs on other people ("She is angry", "She is sad")

4. Helping children to connect their actions to their feelings ("I hit him because I was angry." "I hid because I was afraid.") and to 'talk' about them directly or indirectly through drama, stories, painting, music, etc.

5. Helping children to learn to wait for what they want

6. Helping children to guess the likely outcomes of things they do or say.

7. Helping children to not act on impulse but to stop and think first.

8. Helping children to think of more than one response to a given situation and to choose the one most likely to lead to their desired outcome.

9. Helping children to see a situation from other people's perspective.

With children these skills have to be taught continuously throughout the day. It is not effective to have a slot during the week in which these ideas are discussed in abstract, they have to be incorporated into the very culture of the family or school. A piece of challenging behaviour is then seen as an opportunity to teach self-awareness, a fight between friends an opportunity to practise empathy, a feud in the playground an opportunity to try out mediation skills.

The motivation for these skills to be taught in schools is usually a response to the problem of disruptive behaviour. It is rare that they are put into the context of building an inclusive society, consequently there is still much room for their expansion.

Disability Equality Training

Joining in the spirit of the 1970s when equal opportunities and 'Consciousness Raising' were of great interest to many, disabled people were supported by the Greater London Council to developed our own, user-led method of training. It was designed to give service-providers the means to 'deconstruct' the medical model, understand the social model, and apply this new viewpoint to their particular area of influence or expertise. We called this Disability Equality Training (DET).

DET is not an attempt to help the non-disabled realise how 'awful' it is to be disabled by blindfolding them, or bandaging up their hands, or sticking them in wheelchairs for half-an-hour, with a view to greater 'tolerance' or 'awareness'. It is an attempt to help people realise how their perceptions of disability have become distorted, and to give them a brief insight into our own viewpoint on our situation. The goal is structural change. Through this training we have succeeded in creating a growing awareness amongst many professionals that disability is a human rights issue. We are now taking this tool to Local Education Authorities, parents, schools and young people to help bring about inclusion.

Notes Section Three

1 John McKnight *The Careless Society- Community and its Counterfeits* Basic Books 1995

2 Staff and Pupils of Cleves School, *Learning and Inclusion, The Cleves School Experience*, David Fulton 1998

3 Joe Whittaker, John Kenworthy and Colin Crabtree, *Bolton Data for Inclusion,* Action Research Centre for Inclusion 1998

4 Kenn Jupp, *Everyone Belongs*, Souvenir Press 1992

5 Pupils and Teachers,*Changing Our School*, Highfield Junior School 1997

6 ibid

7 ibid

8 Mary A. Falvey, Marsha Forest, Jack Pearpoint and Richard L. Rosenberg, *All My Life's a Circle: Using the Tools, CIRCLES, MAPS and PATH*, Inclusion Press

9 George Vallient,*Adaption to Life*, Boston, Little and Brown 1977

10 J.K. Felsman and George Vallient, *Resilient Children as Adults, a 40 year Study*, published in *The Invulnerable Child* ed. E.J.Anderson and B.J. Kohles, New York Guilford Press 1987

11 Daniel Goldman, *Emotional Intelligence*, Bloomsbury 1996

12 The Circles Network, *Annual Report* 1996

13 Fritjof Capra,*The Web of Life*, Harper Collins 1996

GLIMPSES OF A POSSIBLE FUTURE

Optimism is not in feeling good, but in believing that good has a chance to survive.

Burton Blatt

My choice is to be optimistic, but I have a good reason to be. I am a disabled person. I represent a group of people who have been systematically devalued and mistreated for hundreds of years, apparently in most (but not all) cultures in the world. We have been thought to be punishments from God, manifestations of sin, the devil's own (foundling) children; we have been left to die on mountains, burnt as witches, cut up and used in medical experiments, forced into institutions, been sterilised en masse, and we have been victims of extermination programmes by Hitler's Third Reich. We have been labelled, segregated and 'screened out' before we are even born.

I feel optimistic because none of it has 'worked'. I live a good and respected life with my own daughter, also a disabled person, within the mainstream, doing meaningful work and in good relation to many people. My daughter and her disabled friends are enjoying a level of respect and support within their mainstream schools which has not been available to any previous generations of disabled young people. I am aware that much of this has been brought about by the efforts of disabled people ourselves, but I can also see that it must be because of the basic desire of human beings to be 'human' that we have been have been supported enough to survive. I can see that sooner or later we will simply be accepted as an important part of the 'whole':

Susie has been my close friend for twenty years, but until 1989, except for me, everyone in her life was similarly disabled or paid to be with her. Having heard about circles from a visitor from the USA, I explained to Susie what I thought they were. The upshot was that Susie asked me to start one for her, although this wasn't easy. Susie was quite definite; she didn't want anyone else with a disability ... and no staff! So we began with some of my friends who she chose.

After a trip to Connecticut I returned fully fired up and really enthusiastic about circles, only to discover that almost everyone had decided to leave the circle. They all had good reasons, unconnected with Susie but I felt afraid of letting her down and ready to give up at this point. Susie decided otherwise. There was Irene, Dorian, Susie and me, and as far as she was concerned, we were going ahead.

Susie invited some of Irenes' friends who she had got to know to join her circle, as well as some more of my friends. Since then the circle has been incredibly strong and has helped Susie achieve some wonderful dreams. The service system had separated Susie from her boyfriend, Colin, and the first thing the circle helped her do was get back together with him again.

The next achievement was when Susie moved from a 24 place hostel to a newly built group home for eight people.

Susie had been attending a day centre which she hated and, using service brokerage, circle members helped re-direct her financial support to buy in job training and support. She managed to get three part-time jobs and organise job coaches, help with transport and the training she needed for the jobs.

Relationships between all the circle members grew. We partied, we strategised, we took action, and we celebrated and commiserated together.

Susie's life continued to change for the better. Colin became her fiance and she moved to a three person house where Colin was also living. Both Susie and Colin were involved in house-hunting with the couple who run the house; they helped in selecting the staff, choosing furniture, deciding on refurbishment and buying birds for the aviary.

With a strong circle and a place to live, Susie now felt safe and ready to start tracking down her family with whom she had lost contact 33 years before. With the help of her college tutor and the couple who ran the house (and had joined the circle), she *finally traced her whole family. Now she has 13 siblings including half-brothers and half-sisters, and with nephews and nieces her family totals 30.*

Now Susie sees her father every week and last year she managed to see her mum just long enough to hold her before she died. Colin also traced his family and discovered two loving sisters who welcome the part he now plays in their lives.

Because the institution where she'd lived hadn't recorded her birthdate correctly, Susie discovered she had been celebrating the wrong date for many years. On her actual 41ˢᵗ birthday, she threw a party for family and friends and so many people came we had to hire a hall.

This year Susie and Colin married and I have never seen her look more happy and radiant.

Mandy Neville – The Circles Network

Meaningful Work For All

If disabled people have learned anything from our appalling history of enforced separation and dependence on service providers, it is that it is a human need to give.

In its broadest aspect, we have not as a society cracked the problem of sharing out the work. Some people are forced to work too hard, and others are pushed into unemployment. The rewards for different types of labour do not correspond to their real value, or indeed to the harm some of them do. "Jobs' are defined in ways which exclude many people, whilst many people make huge contributions to their communities but go unrecognised and unrewarded. Many disabled people are caught in a trap of pretend work in what we have called 'day-wasting centres', the creation of which makes 'real' jobs for the non-disabled managers. Others are doing real work but being denied any financial reward by an irrational benefit system.

Whilst we live in a capitalist system, it is natural that people feel they will be valued by the world when they can make an economic contribution to it. For this reason many disabled people and people with learning difficulties or mental health problems, have fought very hard for the end of discrimination towards us as employees. We have also fought for resources to be made available to us as individuals to buy in the support we need to become economically active.

However, as the demands made by the high-skills, high-wage economy become more insistent, many people are beginning to feel a tremendous conflict between the effort necessary to maintain even a modest standard of living – especially a place to live – and the desire to maintain some sort of quality of life which would include nurturing relationships and having time to be creative.

These conflicts will increase unless we start to re-affirm our basic values and beliefs and create alternative 'models' which put them into practice. The models may well follow examples that are being created in response to the desire to include the 'excluded' into the workforce.

The 'News' is full of isolated incidents of cruelty and violence towards each other, but hardly ever of the thousands upon thousands of daily acts of altruism and kindness, of courage and principled decisions which are what actually enable we fragile and needy human beings to survive at all. Even less do we hear of the instances of groups of people getting together to achieve things which they could not achieve alone. Nor do we begin to acknowledge the dependence of our whole system on voluntary labour without which family life would break down, along with all of our societies, economic and political systems. When the entire picture is taken into account, paid work is but one, over-valued component of community life.

It is interesting that much of the intentional re-building of community initiated by the Inclusion Movement has insisted on the concept of voluntary service at its heart, its heart being at the level of re-building the 'natural' relationships between previously separated people. The people who gather round a person, whether they be a child with a severe impairment, a teenager in 'care', an adult wanting to leave an institution, must do it on a voluntary basis. If they want to bring in paid workers to support a plan, that is fine. It is also fine if the circle is initiated by a person in a paid role, e.g. a teacher, or an advocacy worker, but the members of the group must be there because they want to be, not because it is their job.

The Re-Birth of Public Service

Whilst people who have been excluded from the labour force are challenging their positions, people who are conditioned to think of paid work as their only valid contribution to society are challenging this idea too. Indeed, a growing number of people are realising that most radical work can only happen outside of the labour market, because it challenges the values of the labour market too deeply. For example, parenting. Without the voluntary labour of parents, society could not exist, but parents could never be paid by a capitalist system to do the job. To do so would turn children into 'products' and parents into manufacturers and unconditional love would have nothing to do with it.

The contradictory attitude towards parents of many current Governments highlights the philosophical differences which underpin the struggle towards inclusion. Family values are being loudly promoted in reaction to the disturbing breakdown of family life, whilst at the same time economic policies are forcing mothers to go to work either to 'get off welfare', or to become a house-owner, and for fathers to work long hours in stressful jobs to earn the money to pay for others to 'care' for their dependants.

Many elderly and retired people do in fact donate an enormous amount of time and energy to voluntary service of all kinds, and we still enjoy such things as the Guiding Movement or the Woodcraft Folk, the Lifeboat Institute and many campaigns and associations such as CND or the Ramblers Association, all of which exist because of volunteers. But we do not have a culture which supports and develops the idea of public service, especially amongst young people, creating attitudes which add to the 'uncaring society' they will later inhabit. Inclusive schools help counteract this trend by valuing friendship and support between young people, especially those who rely more than usual on the co-operation of others to survive. It allows young people to feel that they are all needed and can be dependable allies to each other. The evidence is from inclusive schools that this is exactly what young people want.

The Excluded as Leaders

Diversity is a strategic advantage only if there is a truly vibrant community, sustained by a web of relationships. If the community is fragmented into isolated groups and individuals, diversity can easily become a source of prejudice and friction. But if the community is aware of the interdependence of all its members, diversity will enrich the relationships and thus enrich the community as a whole as well as each individual member. In such a community information and ideas flow freely through the entire network, and the diversity of interpretations and learning styles – even the diversity of mistakes, will enrich the entire community.

Fritjof Capra

People who are currently excluded from society, or hidden within, are people who challenge the current world view of human value. When people are not valued, they are not listened to. However, when such people are given the means to represent themselves they are able to provide essential 'feedback' to society.

People who have been excluded have often had a great deal of time and motivation to think about what is needed by society in order to make itself accessible to all. It is one of the most frustrating aspects of the lives of young people, disabled people, and people struggling with emotional distress that our own thinking is not sought when attempts are made to solve our problems. This is not to say we *always* know the answers, or that we never make mistakes, but that our perspective is often the 'missing piece' in the puzzle, the bit that reveals the whole picture. This bit is often the actual cause of the problem - usually an inevitable result of policies and practices which the people trying to solve the problem with their left hands are busy creating with their right hands! - the cause-and-effect which is hard to see without painful self-reflection, but which can be very obvious to the outside observer/victim.

The first move is always going to feel like the hardest. The road to inclusion always starts at the same point of decision in someone's head. *"I will invite people together and ask them to think with me about what we can do"* It is this invitation which changes everything. It feels hard because we are not taught to talk to each other about meaningful things. We are taught to 'chat', be embarrassed, be shy, avoid honesty or vulnerability, hide our feelings, concentrate on trivia, joke around or say what we think people want to hear. We are taught to use alcohol and other drugs to loosen our tongues regardless of the silliness which then comes pouring out. We do not listen because we are too scared to hear. This is why we have developed simple structures that help overcome these problems, and at this point in time these structures have to be taught, or facilitated by someone who knows what they are doing. MAPs, Mediation, Circle Time, peer counselling and Circles of support are all organised forms of making our interdependence conscious. It is the use of these 'tools' which stops the lip-service paid to 'Inclusion' and starts the real journey.

There is no point in building an inclusive education system unless it leads to an 'inclusive' life as an adult. This means that not only do children's services need to be restructured, but all services including housing, town and country planning, transport, employment, social and health services and even our funding systems

Planning Our Destinies

I have sometimes been tempted into thinking that it would be nice to follow the 'alternative trail', to give up the struggle and go and live a simple life away from the jungle. The idea of wigwams in Wales and growing our own food has great appeal, until I am brought up short by a dreadful question -WHERE WOULD I PLUG IN MY ELECTRIC WHEELCHAIR?! The nice warm feeling dissolves into great angst as I imagine having to be carried across muddy fields every time I wanted to move somewhere or talk to someone. No, technology and development are not in themselves all bad. Indeed, disabled people are probably the best example of being empowered by technical means - speech synthesisers, powered chairs, Braille-converting software, user-operated environmental systems all have transformed our lives. The problem is about whose needs are being served, a mindless system based on greed, or people, and our desire to live well on a planet of finite resources.

There are many people engaged in trying to find answers to these questions, I know. The environmental movement, new economics movement, the peace movement, those trying to protect our wildlife, and all those working towards the end of oppression and injustice. The great religions are still struggling to think about the meaning of life and how to live it, scientists are still seeking to understand how to solve our technical problems, including those we have created ourselves; many philosophers and psychologists are still seeking to find out what constitutes human nature, and I know that even doctors are doing their best to end unnecessary pain and disease.

The reason I think this inclusion movement is not just one of many, is that I think it offers a short-cut for all of us to start to act decisively to end human suffering. By recognising that putting the most de-valued and least understood human beings back in the centre of our lives, by supporting the creation of inclusive schools, joining circles of support, making the time to listen to each other think and 'dream', giving up pretence that we don't need each other, using paid service providers to support relationships and community, inviting a 'difficult' child round to tea, learning to identify the gifts we all bring, removing the barriers to participation we have unawarely created, we will create the safety we all need to design the solutions to the big, global problems we have. If, however, we continue to think that we can leave these people to last because other issues are more pressing or important, I do not think we will ever learn enough about human nature to be able to take control of our own lives, or to understand the consequences of our own actions. The global community will fragment and become more unstable and isolation and fear will continue to run our lives.

A World Wide Change Programme

In my view, what is needed is a world wide change programme based on the principles of inclusion.

The underlying principles need to recognise that each and every human being has a right to life, to respect and to the means of participation in their societies. It would recognise that the oppressive society hurts everyone - perpetrators and victims; that we can heal our hurts; that we can solve our problems; that the voices of the excluded must be heard, that we all bring gifts to share, that diversity is necessary to maintain living systems, that it takes time to think, that friendship is fundamental, and that communities must be centred around creating safety for their most vulnerable members.

This programme would need to include:

- ❖ **The recognition that a persons worth is independent of their abilities or achievements**
- ❖ **The aware recognition of our interdependence**
- ❖ **The design of a workable economic system based on the needs of people, not profit.**
- ❖ **Inclusive education world-wide**
- ❖ **A redefinition of work**
- ❖ **A redefinition of health**
- ❖ **A redefinition of intelligence**
- ❖ **An anti-Eugenics policy**
- ❖ **The reclamation of technology to serve our real needs**
- ❖ **A social wage for those who want it**
- ❖ **The protection and healing of our physical environment**
- ❖ **The intentional re-building of communities**
- ❖ **Multilateral disarmament**
- ❖ **A universal means of communication between peoples**
- ❖ **The valuing of public service**

This book is partly a rallying call. I believe there are many people out there who are longing to work together to bring this 'dream' into reality. If you are one of them please get in touch with me at:

The Alliance for Inclusive Education
Unit 2,
70 South Lambeth Road,
London SW8 IRL

Or by E-Mail to Micheline@michathome.supanet.com

or by joining our E-mail discussion list by subscribing to
inclusionuk@onelist.com

TOGETHER WE ARE BETTER.

Guildford College
Learning Resource Centre

Please return on or before the last date shown.
No further issues or renewals if any items are overdue.
"7 Day" loans are **NOT** renewable.

Class: 361. 61 MAS

Title: Incurably Human

Author: Mason, Micheline.